Table of Contents

Chapter 1: Introduction to Kotlin and Android Development

1.1 Getting Started with Kotlin

Kotlin is a modern, statically-typed programming language that has gained popularity for Android app development. It offers many advantages over Java, the traditional language for Android development, including concise syntax, null safety, and enhanced support for functional programming. In this section, we will guide you through the process of getting started with Kotlin for Android development.

Installing Kotlin

To begin using Kotlin for Android development, you need to install the Kotlin programming language. Here are the steps for installing Kotlin on different platforms:

Installing Kotlin on Windows

1. Download the Kotlin Compiler (kotlinc) for Windows.
2. Run the installer and follow the on-screen instructions to complete the installation.
3. Once installed, open a command prompt and type kotlinc to verify that Kotlin is correctly installed.

Installing Kotlin on Mac

1. You can use Homebrew to install Kotlin on macOS. Open a terminal and run the following command:

```
brew install kotlin
```

2. After the installation is complete, you can check the Kotlin version by typing kotlin -version in the terminal.

Installing Kotlin on Linux

1. On Linux, you can use SDKMAN to manage Kotlin installations. First, install SDKMAN with the following command:

```
curl -s "https://get.sdkman.io" | bash
```

2. After installing SDKMAN, use it to install Kotlin:

```
sdk install kotlin
```

3. Verify the Kotlin installation by running kotlin -version.

Writing Your First Kotlin Android Project

Now that you have Kotlin installed, it's time to create your first Android project. You can use Android Studio, the official IDE for Android development, to create a new Kotlin-based Android application. Follow these steps:

1. Open Android Studio and click on "Start a new Android Studio project."

2. Choose a project template, configure your project settings, and click "Finish."

3. Android Studio will generate a basic Kotlin Android app for you to start with. You can explore the project structure, which includes Kotlin source files, XML layout files, and resource files.

4. You can write your Kotlin code in the `.kt` files within the `src` directory of your project. Android Studio provides code completion and many helpful features to make development easier.

5. To run your app, connect an Android device or use an emulator, then click the "Run" button in Android Studio.

Congratulations! You've successfully set up Kotlin for Android development and created your first Kotlin-based Android app. In the following sections, we will dive deeper into Kotlin's syntax and Android development concepts.

This is just the beginning of your journey into Android app development with Kotlin. In the upcoming chapters, we'll explore Kotlin's core features, Android UI development, data persistence, networking, and much more. So, let's get started and build amazing Android apps with Kotlin!

1.2 Setting Up Kotlin on Windows

Setting up Kotlin on Windows is a crucial step in your journey toward Android app development using this versatile programming language. In this section, we will walk you through the process of configuring your Windows environment for Kotlin development.

Installing Java Development Kit (JDK)

Before you can work with Kotlin, you need to have the Java Development Kit (JDK) installed on your Windows machine. Kotlin is compatible with JDK 8, 11, or later. Here's how to install JDK:

1. Visit the Oracle JDK download page or the OpenJDK website to download the JDK installer for Windows.

2. Run the installer and follow the on-screen instructions to complete the installation. Make sure to remember the installation path, as you will need it later.

3. To verify the installation, open a command prompt and type the following command:

   ```
   java -version
   ```

   You should see information about the installed Java version.

Installing Kotlin

Once you have the JDK installed, you can proceed to install Kotlin:

1. Download the Kotlin Compiler (kotlinc) for Windows from the official Kotlin releases page.

2. Run the installer and follow the installation steps. You will be prompted to choose the installation directory. You can select the default location or specify a custom one.

3. After the installation is complete, open a command prompt and type the following command to check if Kotlin is correctly installed:

   ```
   kotlinc -version
   ```

   This should display the Kotlin version information, indicating that Kotlin is ready for use.

Configuring Environment Variables

To make it easier to work with Kotlin and Java, you can configure environment variables. Here's how to do it:

1. Right-click on "This PC" or "My Computer" and select "Properties."

2. Click on "Advanced system settings" on the left-hand side.

3. In the "System Properties" window, click the "Environment Variables" button.

4. In the "System Variables" section, find the "Path" variable and click "Edit."

5. Add the paths to the Kotlin and JDK binaries. Typically, these paths will be something like:

   ```
   -   C:\Program Files\kotlin\bin
   -   C:\Program Files\Java\jdk1.x.x_xxx\bin
   ```
   Replace x.x_xxx with the actual version of your JDK.

6. Click "OK" to save the changes.

With these environment variables set up, you can easily access Kotlin and Java from the command line without specifying the full path to their executables each time.

Now that you've successfully set up Kotlin on your Windows machine, you're ready to start writing Kotlin code and developing Android applications using this powerful language. In the next sections, we'll explore more Kotlin features and Android development concepts to help you build amazing apps.

1.3 Setting Up Kotlin on Mac

Configuring Kotlin on a Mac is a fundamental step in preparing your development environment for Android app development using Kotlin. In this section, we will guide you through the process of setting up Kotlin on macOS.

Installing Java Development Kit (JDK)

Before you can work with Kotlin, it's essential to have the Java Development Kit (JDK) installed on your Mac. Kotlin is compatible with JDK 8, 11, or later. Here's how to install JDK on macOS:

1. Visit the Oracle JDK download page or the OpenJDK website to download the JDK installer for macOS.

2. Run the installer and follow the on-screen instructions to complete the installation. Make sure to remember the installation path, as you will need it later.

3. To verify the installation, open a terminal and type the following command:

   ```
   java -version
   ```

   You should see information about the installed Java version.

Installing Kotlin

Once you have the JDK installed, you can proceed to install Kotlin on your Mac:

1. You can use Homebrew, a popular package manager for macOS, to install Kotlin. Open a terminal and run the following command to install Homebrew if you haven't already:

   ```
   /bin/bash -c "$(curl -fsSL https://raw.githubusercontent.com/Homebrew/install/master/install.sh)"
   ```

2. After installing Homebrew, you can use it to install Kotlin by running the following command:

   ```
   brew install kotlin
   ```

3. After the installation is complete, you can check the Kotlin version by typing the following command in the terminal:

   ```
   kotlinc -version
   ```

   This should display the Kotlin version information, confirming that Kotlin is ready for use.

To streamline your Kotlin and Java development experience on macOS, you can configure environment variables. Here's how to do it:

1. Open a terminal.

2. Use a text editor like Nano or Vim to edit your shell profile file. For example:

    ```
    nano ~/.zshrc  # If you're using the Zsh shell
    ```

3. Add the paths to the Kotlin and JDK binaries by adding the following lines to your shell profile file. Modify the paths as needed:

    ```
    export PATH="$PATH:/usr/local/bin/kotlin"
    export JAVA_HOME="/Library/Java/JavaVirtualMachines/jdk-x.x.x_xxx/Conte
    nts/Home"  # Replace with the actual JDK path
    ```

    Replace x.x.x_xxx with the actual version of your JDK.

4. Save the file and exit the text editor.

5. Apply the changes to your current terminal session by running:

    ```
    source ~/.zshrc  # or source your respective shell profile file
    ```

With these environment variables set up, you can easily access Kotlin and Java from the terminal without specifying the full path to their executables each time.

Now that you've successfully configured Kotlin on your Mac, you're ready to start coding in Kotlin and building Android apps using this versatile language. In the upcoming sections, we'll delve deeper into Kotlin and Android development concepts to help you become proficient in creating Android applications.

1.4 Setting Up Kotlin on Linux

Setting up Kotlin on a Linux system is a crucial step to prepare your development environment for Android app development using Kotlin. In this section, we will guide you through the process of setting up Kotlin on a Linux-based operating system.

Installing Java Development Kit (JDK)

Before you can work with Kotlin, it's essential to have the Java Development Kit (JDK) installed on your Linux machine. Kotlin is compatible with JDK 8, 11, or later. Here's how to install JDK on Linux:

If you're using a Debian-based Linux distribution like Ubuntu, you can use the package manager to install the JDK. Open a terminal and run the following commands:

```
sudo apt update
sudo apt install default-jdk
```

This will install the default JDK available for your distribution.

Using Package Manager (Fedora/CentOS)

If you're using a Red Hat-based distribution like Fedora or CentOS, you can use the package manager to install the JDK. Open a terminal and run the following commands:

```
sudo dnf install java-11-openjdk-devel  # For JDK 11, adjust the version as needed
```

Downloading from Oracle or OpenJDK

Alternatively, you can download the JDK directly from the Oracle JDK download page or the OpenJDK website and follow the installation instructions provided on their respective websites.

To verify the installation, open a terminal and type the following command:

```
java -version
```

You should see information about the installed Java version.

Installing Kotlin

Once you have the JDK installed, you can proceed to install Kotlin on your Linux system. Here's how to do it:

Using SDKMAN

SDKMAN is a convenient tool for managing software development kits, including Kotlin, on Linux. Follow these steps:

1. Open a terminal and run the following command to install SDKMAN:
```
curl -s "https://get.sdkman.io" | bash
```

2. After the installation is complete, restart your terminal or run:
```
source "$HOME/.sdkman/bin/sdkman-init.sh"
```

3. Now, you can use SDKMAN to install Kotlin:
```
sdk install kotlin
```

4. To verify the Kotlin installation, run:
```
kotlin -version
```

Alternatively, you can download the Kotlin Compiler (kotlinc) for Linux from the official Kotlin releases page. After downloading, follow these steps:

1. Extract the downloaded archive to a location of your choice.

2. Add the Kotlin bin directory to your system's PATH. You can do this by editing your shell profile file, such as `.bashrc` or `.zshrc`, and adding the following line (replace `path/to/kotlinc/bin` with the actual path):

```
export PATH="$PATH:/path/to/kotlinc/bin"
```

3. Save the file and source it in your terminal:

```
source ~/.bashrc   # or source your respective shell profile file
```

With Kotlin successfully installed on your Linux machine, you're ready to start coding in Kotlin and building Android apps using this powerful language. In the upcoming sections, we'll delve deeper into Kotlin and Android development concepts to help you become proficient in creating Android applications.

1.5 Your First Android Project in Kotlin

Congratulations on setting up Kotlin on your development environment! Now it's time to create your first Android project using Kotlin. In this section, we will guide you through the process of creating a simple Android application to get you started.

Using Android Studio

Android Studio is the official Integrated Development Environment (IDE) for Android app development. It provides powerful tools and features to streamline the development process. Here's how to create your first Kotlin-based Android project using Android Studio:

1. **Open Android Studio**: Launch Android Studio on your computer.

2. **Start a New Project**: Click on "Start a new Android Studio project" or go to `File -> New -> New Project`.

3. **Choose a Template**: Select the "Empty Activity" template to create a minimal Android app.

4. **Configure Your Project**:

    - Enter a name for your project.
    - Choose a package name for your app (usually in reverse domain format, like `com.example.myfirstapp`).
    - Select the language as "Kotlin."

5. **Configure Additional Settings**:

- Choose the minimum API level for your app. This determines the lowest Android version your app will support.
- You can leave other settings as default for now.

6. **Finish Project Setup**: Click the "Finish" button to create your project.

Once your project is created, you'll see a project structure in Android Studio's Project pane on the left. Here's a brief overview of the key components:

- **app**: This is where your app's main code resides. Look under `app/src/main` for Kotlin source files, layout XML files, and other resources.

- **res**: This directory contains resources such as layout files, strings, and drawables.

- **Manifests**: The `AndroidManifest.xml` file defines essential information about your app, including its activities, permissions, and more.

- **Gradle Scripts**: The `build.gradle` files define project and module-level dependencies and settings.

Now let's write some Kotlin code for your first Android app. Open the `MainActivity.kt` file under `app/src/main/java/com/example/myfirstapp` (replace `com.example.myfirstapp` with your actual package name).

Here's a simple example that displays a "Hello, World!" message when the app starts:

```kotlin
package com.example.myfirstapp

import androidx.appcompat.app.AppCompatActivity
import android.os.Bundle
import android.widget.TextView

class MainActivity : AppCompatActivity() {
    override fun onCreate(savedInstanceState: Bundle?) {
        super.onCreate(savedInstanceState)
        setContentView(R.layout.activity_main)

        // Find the TextView by its ID
        val textView: TextView = findViewById(R.id.textView)

        // Set the text of the TextView
        textView.text = "Hello, World!"
    }
}
```

Designing the User Interface

To design the user interface, open the `activity_main.xml` layout file under `app/src/main/res/layout`. You can use the visual layout editor in Android Studio to drag and drop UI elements or edit the XML directly. Here's an example XML layout that includes a TextView:

```xml
<?xml version="1.0" encoding="utf-8"?>
<RelativeLayout xmlns:android="http://schemas.android.com/apk/res/android"
    xmlns:app="http://schemas.android.com/apk/res-auto"
    xmlns:tools="http://schemas.android.com/tools"
    android:layout_width="match_parent"
    android:layout_height="match_parent"
    android:padding="16dp"
    tools:context=".MainActivity">

    <TextView
        android:id="@+id/textView"
        android:layout_width="wrap_content"
        android:layout_height="wrap_content"
        android:text="Hello, World!"
        android:textSize="24sp"
        android:layout_centerInParent="true" />
</RelativeLayout>
```

Running Your App

Now it's time to run your app. Connect an Android device to your computer or create a virtual device using the Android Emulator. Then, click the "Run" button in Android Studio. Your app will be installed and launched on the selected device or emulator.

You should see the "Hello, World!" message displayed on the screen.

Congratulations! You've created your first Android app using Kotlin and Android Studio. This is just the beginning of your journey into Android app development. In the upcoming chapters, we'll explore more advanced topics and help you build feature-rich Android applications.

Chapter 2: Kotlin Basics for Android

2.1 Variables and Data Types in Kotlin

In Kotlin, like in many programming languages, variables are used to store and manage data. Understanding variables and data types is fundamental for any programming task. In this section, we will explore how to declare variables, assign values to them, and the different data types available in Kotlin.

Declaring Variables

To declare a variable in Kotlin, you use the `val` or `var` keyword followed by the variable name. Here's a basic example:

```
val name: String = "John"
var age: Int = 30
```

- `val` is used for read-only (immutable) variables. Once you assign a value to a `val`, you cannot change it.
- `var` is used for mutable variables. You can change the value assigned to a `var`.

In the example above, we declared two variables, `name` and `age`, and specified their data types (`String` and `Int`, respectively).

Data Types

Kotlin provides a variety of data types to work with different kinds of data. Here are some common data types:

- `Int`: Represents whole numbers (e.g., 1, 42, -3).
- `Long`: Represents long integers (e.g., 123456789L).
- `Float`: Represents floating-point numbers (e.g., 3.14f).
- `Double`: Represents double-precision floating-point numbers (e.g., 2.71828).
- `Char`: Represents a single character (e.g., 'A', '1').
- `Boolean`: Represents true or false values.
- `String`: Represents a sequence of characters (e.g., "Hello, Kotlin!").

Type Inference

Kotlin has a feature called "type inference," which allows the compiler to automatically determine the data type of a variable based on its value. This means you can often omit the explicit data type when declaring a variable, and Kotlin will infer it for you:

```
val name = "Alice" // Kotlin infers String
var count = 42     // Kotlin infers Int
```

Variable Naming Rules

When naming variables in Kotlin, you should follow these rules:

- Variable names are case-sensitive.
- Variable names must start with a letter or an underscore.
- Variable names can include letters, digits, and underscores.
- Variable names cannot contain spaces or special characters (except underscores).

Initializing Variables

In Kotlin, you can declare a variable without initializing it immediately. However, you must initialize it before using it. Kotlin provides a null value to indicate the absence of a value. Here's an example:

```kotlin
var phoneNumber: String? // Declare a nullable String
phoneNumber = null       // Initialize with null
```

In this case, phoneNumber is declared as a nullable String (String?), and it can either contain a string value or be null.

Type Conversion

Kotlin provides automatic type conversion for compatible data types, but you may need to perform explicit type conversion (also known as "casting") in some cases. Here's an example of type conversion:

```kotlin
val num1: Int = 42
val num2: Double = num1.toDouble() // Explicitly convert Int to Double
```

In this example, we use the toDouble() function to convert an Int to a Double.

Understanding variables and data types is the foundation of writing Kotlin code. In the upcoming sections, we'll explore control flow, functions, and more advanced Kotlin concepts to help you become proficient in Android app development with Kotlin.

2.2 Control Flow and Conditional Statements

Control flow in programming allows you to make decisions, repeat actions, and create complex logic in your code. Conditional statements, such as if, else if, and when in Kotlin, enable you to control the flow of your program based on specific conditions.

The if Expression

The if expression is used to execute a block of code if a condition is true. It has the following syntax:

```kotlin
if (condition) {
    // Code to execute when the condition is true
```

```
} else {
    // Code to execute when the condition is false
}
```

Here's a simple example:

```
val num = 10

if (num > 5) {
    println("Number is greater than 5")
} else {
    println("Number is not greater than 5")
}
```

In this example, if num is greater than 5, the message "Number is greater than 5" is printed; otherwise, "Number is not greater than 5" is printed.

The else if Clause

You can use the else if clause to check multiple conditions sequentially. Here's the syntax:

```
if (condition1) {
    // Code to execute when condition1 is true
} else if (condition2) {
    // Code to execute when condition2 is true
} else {
    // Code to execute when no conditions are true
}
```

Here's an example:

```
val grade = 85

if (grade >= 90) {
    println("A")
} else if (grade >= 80) {
    println("B")
} else if (grade >= 70) {
    println("C")
} else {
    println("F")
}
```

In this example, the code determines the grade based on the value of grade.

The when Expression

The when expression is a versatile way to perform conditional checks in Kotlin. It is similar to a switch statement in other programming languages. Here's the basic syntax:

```kotlin
when (value) {
    case1 -> {
        // Code to execute when value equals case1
    }
    case2, case3 -> {
        // Code to execute when value equals case2 or case3
    }
    else -> {
        // Code to execute when no cases match
    }
}
```

Here's an example:

```kotlin
val day = "Wednesday"

when (day) {
    "Monday" -> println("Start of the workweek")
    "Tuesday" -> println("Second day of the week")
    "Wednesday" -> println("Hump day!")
    else -> println("Weekday")
}
```

In this example, when checks the value of day and prints a message based on the day of the week.

Conditional Operators

Kotlin also provides conditional operators for concise conditional expressions. For example, the Elvis operator (?:) allows you to provide a default value when a variable is null:

```kotlin
val result = someValue ?: defaultValue
```

The Safe Call operator (?.) allows you to safely access properties or call methods on nullable objects without causing a `NullPointerException`:

```kotlin
val length = text?.length
```

These operators can make your code more concise and safe when dealing with nullable values.

Understanding control flow and conditional statements is essential for creating dynamic and responsive Kotlin code. In the next sections, we'll explore loops and iterations, functions, and more advanced concepts to help you become proficient in Android app development with Kotlin.

2.3 Loops and Iterations

Loops are essential for repeating a specific task or executing a block of code multiple times. In Kotlin, you can use several types of loops to control the flow of your program. In this section, we'll explore the for, while, and do-while loops.

The for Loop

The for loop in Kotlin allows you to iterate over a range, a collection, or any iterable object. Here's the basic syntax:

```
for (variable in iterable) {
    // Code to execute in each iteration
}
```

Here's an example of iterating through a range of numbers:

```
for (i in 1..5) {
    println("Number: $i")
}
```

In this example, the loop iterates from 1 to 5, and the value of i changes in each iteration.

You can also use a for loop to iterate over elements in a collection:

```
val fruits = listOf("Apple", "Banana", "Cherry")

for (fruit in fruits) {
    println("Fruit: $fruit")
}
```

The while Loop

The while loop in Kotlin allows you to repeatedly execute a block of code as long as a given condition is true. Here's the syntax:

```
while (condition) {
    // Code to execute while the condition is true
}
```

Here's an example of a while loop:

```
var count = 0

while (count < 5) {
    println("Count: $count")
    count++
}
```

In this example, the loop continues as long as `count` is less than 5. The `count` variable is incremented in each iteration.

The `do-while` Loop

The `do-while` loop is similar to the `while` loop, but it guarantees that the code block is executed at least once before checking the condition. Here's the syntax:

```
do {
    // Code to execute at least once
} while (condition)
```

Here's an example:

```
var number = 5

do {
    println("Number: $number")
    number--
} while (number > 0)
```

In this example, the code block is executed once even though `number` is initially 5 because the condition is checked after the first execution.

Loop Control Statements

Kotlin provides loop control statements to modify the behavior of loops. These include:

- break: Terminates the loop prematurely.
- continue: Skips the current iteration and proceeds to the next one.
- return: Exits the entire function containing the loop.

Here's an example of using break to exit a loop early:

```
for (i in 1..10) {
    if (i == 5) {
        println("Breaking the loop")
        break
    }
    println("Number: $i")
}
```

In this example, the loop breaks when i becomes 5.

Loops are powerful tools for handling repetitive tasks and iterating over data structures. Understanding how to use `for`, `while`, and `do-while` loops, as well as loop control statements, is crucial for writing efficient and flexible Kotlin code. In the following sections, we'll explore functions, exception handling, and more advanced Kotlin concepts to enhance your Android app development skills.

2.4 Functions and Lambdas in Kotlin

Functions are fundamental building blocks in programming that allow you to encapsulate a block of code with a specific purpose and reuse it as needed. Kotlin provides powerful support for defining functions and working with lambdas, which are anonymous functions. In this section, we'll explore functions and lambdas in Kotlin.

Defining Functions

In Kotlin, you can define functions using the `fun` keyword. Here's the basic syntax of a function:

```kotlin
fun functionName(parameters: ParameterType): ReturnType {
    // Code to execute
    return returnValue
}
```

Here's a simple example of a function that calculates the sum of two numbers:

```kotlin
fun sum(a: Int, b: Int): Int {
    return a + b
}
```

You can call this function by providing arguments, like this:

```kotlin
val result = sum(5, 3)
println("Sum: $result")
```

Default Arguments

Kotlin allows you to specify default values for function parameters, making it convenient to call functions with fewer arguments when needed. Here's an example:

```kotlin
fun greet(name: String = "Guest") {
    println("Hello, $name!")
}

greet("Alice") // Prints: Hello, Alice!
greet()        // Prints: Hello, Guest!
```

In this example, the `name` parameter has a default value of "Guest," so you can call `greet()` without providing an argument.

Named Arguments

Kotlin supports named arguments, allowing you to specify the parameter name when calling a function. This can make function calls more readable, especially for functions with many parameters:

```kotlin
fun createPerson(name: String, age: Int, city: String) {
    // Code to create a person
}

createPerson(name = "Bob", age = 30, city = "New York")
```

Lambdas and Higher-Order Functions

Lambdas are anonymous functions that can be passed as arguments to other functions. Kotlin allows you to define lambdas concisely using a lambda expression. Here's an example of a lambda expression that squares a number:

```kotlin
val square: (Int) -> Int = { x -> x * x }
val result = square(5) // result is 25
```

In this example, square is a lambda that takes an Int as input and returns an Int.

Kotlin also supports higher-order functions, which are functions that can accept other functions as arguments or return functions as results. This allows you to write more expressive and flexible code. Here's an example:

```kotlin
fun operateOnNumbers(a: Int, b: Int, operation: (Int, Int) -> Int): Int {
    return operation(a, b)
}

val addition: (Int, Int) -> Int = { x, y -> x + y }
val subtraction: (Int, Int) -> Int = { x, y -> x - y }

val result1 = operateOnNumbers(5, 3, addition)       // result1 is 8
val result2 = operateOnNumbers(10, 4, subtraction) // result2 is 6
```

In this example, operateOnNumbers is a higher-order function that takes two numbers and an operation function as arguments.

Extension Functions

Kotlin allows you to extend existing classes with new functionality by defining extension functions. Extension functions are defined outside the class they extend but can be called as if they were member functions of the class. Here's an example:

```kotlin
fun String.reverse(): String {
    return this.reversed()
}

val reversedText = "Kotlin".reverse() // reversedText is "niltK"
```

In this example, we define an extension function reverse for the String class, allowing us to reverse the contents of a string easily.

Functions and lambdas are essential components of Kotlin, enabling you to create modular, reusable, and expressive code. In the upcoming sections, we'll explore more advanced

Kotlin concepts, including object-oriented programming, Android-specific topics, and best practices for Android app development.

2.5 Exception Handling in Kotlin

Exception handling is a critical aspect of programming, as it allows you to gracefully handle errors and unexpected situations that may occur during the execution of your code. In Kotlin, exception handling is done using try-catch blocks. In this section, we'll explore how to handle exceptions in Kotlin.

The try-catch Block

The `try-catch` block in Kotlin is used to encapsulate code that may throw exceptions. It allows you to catch and handle exceptions, preventing them from crashing your application. Here's the basic syntax:

```kotlin
try {
    // Code that may throw an exception
} catch (exceptionType: Exception) {
    // Code to handle the exception
}
```

Here's an example of a `try-catch` block that handles a `NumberFormatException`:

```kotlin
fun convertToInteger(value: String): Int {
    return try {
        value.toInt()
    } catch (e: NumberFormatException) {
        // Handle the exception
        println("Invalid number format")
        0 // Return a default value
    }
}

val result = convertToInteger("123")
```

In this example, the `convertToInteger` function attempts to convert a string to an integer using `toInt()`. If the conversion fails due to an invalid number format, the `catch` block is executed, and a default value of 0 is returned.

Multiple catch Blocks

You can have multiple `catch` blocks to handle different types of exceptions. Kotlin will execute the first `catch` block that matches the thrown exception type. Here's an example:

```kotlin
fun divide(a: Int, b: Int): Int {
    return try {
        a / b
    } catch (e: ArithmeticException) {
```

```
        println("ArithmeticException: Division by zero")
        0
    } catch (e: Exception) {
        println("Generic Exception: ${e.message}")
        1
    }
}
```

```
val result = divide(10, 0)
```

In this example, the `divide` function attempts to perform division, and it has two `catch` blocks—one for `ArithmeticException` and another for `Exception`. The first `catch` block will handle division by zero errors, while the second one will catch any other exceptions.

The `finally` Block

In addition to `try` and `catch`, Kotlin provides the `finally` block, which is used to specify code that should be executed regardless of whether an exception is thrown or not. Here's an example:

```
fun readFile(filename: String): String {
    return try {
        // Read the file
        "File contents"
    } catch (e: Exception) {
        println("Error reading the file: ${e.message}")
        ""
    } finally {
        println("Closing file")
        // Close the file or perform cleanup
    }
}
```

In this example, the `finally` block ensures that the file is closed or cleanup operations are performed, even if an exception occurs during file reading.

Custom Exceptions

In addition to handling built-in exceptions, you can create custom exceptions in Kotlin by defining your own exception classes. This can be useful for signaling and handling application-specific errors. Here's a basic example:

```
class CustomException(message: String) : Exception(message)
```

```
fun process(data: String) {
    if (data.isEmpty()) {
        throw CustomException("Data cannot be empty")
    }
    // Process the data
}
```

In this example, we define a custom exception `CustomException`. If the `process` function receives empty data, it throws this custom exception with a specific message.

Exception handling is a crucial part of writing robust and reliable Kotlin code. By using `try-catch` blocks and custom exceptions, you can gracefully handle errors and ensure that your Android app remains stable and responsive even when unexpected issues arise. In the upcoming chapters, we'll explore more advanced Android-specific topics and best practices for Kotlin app development.

Chapter 3: Object-Oriented Programming in Kotlin

3.1 Classes and Objects in Kotlin

Object-oriented programming (OOP) is a programming paradigm that focuses on organizing code into objects, which represent real-world entities. In Kotlin, classes and objects are fundamental constructs for implementing OOP principles. In this section, we'll explore how to define classes, create objects, and work with properties and methods.

Defining Classes

In Kotlin, you can define a class using the `class` keyword. Here's the basic syntax:

```kotlin
class ClassName {
    // Properties and methods go here
}
```

Here's a simple example of a `Person` class with properties for name and age:

```kotlin
class Person {
    var name: String = ""
    var age: Int = 0
}
```

Creating Objects

Once you've defined a class, you can create objects (instances) of that class. To create an object, use the class name followed by parentheses. Here's an example of creating two Person objects:

```kotlin
val person1 = Person()
val person2 = Person()
```

Properties

Classes in Kotlin can have properties, which are essentially variables that belong to an object. You can access and modify properties of an object using dot notation. Here's an example:

```kotlin
val person = Person()
person.name = "Alice"
person.age = 30
```

In this example, we create a `Person` object and set its name and age properties.

Constructors

Kotlin allows you to define one or more constructors for a class. A constructor is a special function called when an object is created. The primary constructor is defined in the class header, and secondary constructors are defined using the `constructor` keyword. Here's an example of a primary constructor:

```kotlin
class Person(val name: String, val age: Int)
```

You can create a `Person` object and pass values to the constructor like this:

```kotlin
val person = Person("Bob", 25)
```

Methods

Classes can also have methods, which are functions associated with objects of the class. Here's an example of a `Person` class with a method:

```kotlin
class Person(val name: String, val age: Int) {
    fun greet() {
        println("Hello, my name is $name and I'm $age years old.")
    }
}
```

You can call the greet method on a `Person` object:

```kotlin
val person = Person("Carol", 35)
person.greet() // Prints: Hello, my name is Carol and I'm 35 years old.
```

Inheritance

Inheritance is a fundamental OOP concept that allows you to create a new class based on an existing class. In Kotlin, you can use the : `SuperClass()` syntax to declare inheritance. Here's an example:

```kotlin
open class Animal(val name: String)

class Dog(name: String) : Animal(name)
```

In this example, the `Dog` class inherits from the `Animal` class. The open keyword is used to allow other classes to inherit from `Animal`.

Overriding Methods

When you inherit from a class, you can override its methods in the subclass. Use the override keyword to indicate that a method is intended to replace a method with the same signature in the superclass. Here's an example:

```kotlin
open class Animal {
    open fun speak() {
        println("Animal speaks")
    }
}

class Dog : Animal() {
    override fun speak() {
```

```
        println("Dog barks")
    }
}
```

In this example, the Dog class overrides the speak method from the Animal class.

Encapsulation

Encapsulation is the practice of restricting access to certain parts of an object and exposing only the necessary details. In Kotlin, you can use access modifiers like public, private, protected, and internal to control access to properties and methods. Here's an example:

```
class MyClass {
    private val privateProperty = 42

    fun accessPrivateProperty() {
        println(privateProperty)
    }
}
```

In this example, privateProperty can only be accessed within the MyClass class.

Understanding classes, objects, and object-oriented programming principles is essential for building structured and maintainable Kotlin code. In the following sections, we'll explore more advanced OOP concepts in Kotlin, including inheritance, interfaces, and design patterns.

3.2 Inheritance and Polymorphism

Inheritance is a fundamental concept in object-oriented programming that allows you to create new classes based on existing classes. It promotes code reuse and establishes relationships between classes, where a derived class (subclass) inherits properties and behaviors from a base class (superclass). In Kotlin, you can achieve inheritance using the : syntax. This section explores inheritance and the concept of polymorphism in Kotlin.

Inheritance in Kotlin

To create a subclass that inherits from a superclass in Kotlin, you use the : symbol followed by the name of the superclass in the class declaration. Here's a basic example:

```
open class Animal(val name: String) {
    open fun makeSound() {
        println("The animal makes a sound")
    }
}

class Dog(name: String) : Animal(name) {
    override fun makeSound() {
```

```kotlin
        println("The dog barks")
    }
}
```

In this example, the Dog class inherits from the Animal class. The open keyword is used to indicate that the Animal class and its makeSound method can be overridden in subclasses. The Dog class overrides the makeSound method to provide a specific implementation.

Polymorphism

Polymorphism is a key concept in OOP that allows objects of different classes to be treated as objects of a common superclass. In Kotlin, polymorphism is achieved through method overriding and interfaces. Here's an example of how polymorphism works:

```kotlin
fun main() {
    val animals: Array<Animal> = arrayOf(Animal("Lion"), Dog("Fido"))

    for (animal in animals) {
        println("${animal.name}:")
        animal.makeSound()
    }
}
```

In this code, we create an array of Animal objects that includes both Animal and Dog instances. When we iterate through the array and call the makeSound method on each object, the appropriate makeSound implementation is executed based on the actual type of the object. This is an example of runtime polymorphism.

Superclass Constructors

When a subclass inherits from a superclass, it needs to call the superclass's constructor to initialize the inherited properties and perform any necessary setup. In Kotlin, you can call the superclass constructor using the super keyword. Here's an example:

```kotlin
open class Animal(val name: String) {
    open fun makeSound() {
        println("The animal makes a sound")
    }
}

class Dog(name: String) : Animal(name) {
    override fun makeSound() {
        println("The dog barks")
    }

    fun playFetch() {
        println("The dog plays fetch")
    }
}
```

In this example, the `Dog` class calls the `Animal` constructor with the `name` parameter using `super(name)`.

In some cases, you may want to define a superclass that cannot be instantiated directly. Kotlin provides the `abstract` keyword for this purpose. Abstract classes cannot be instantiated on their own but can be inherited by other classes that provide concrete implementations for their abstract methods. Here's an example:

```kotlin
abstract class Shape {
    abstract fun calculateArea(): Double
}

class Circle(val radius: Double) : Shape() {
    override fun calculateArea(): Double {
        return Math.PI * radius * radius
    }
}
```

In this example, the `Shape` class is abstract and has an abstract method `calculateArea()`. The `Circle` class inherits from `Shape` and provides a concrete implementation for `calculateArea()`.

Understanding inheritance and polymorphism is essential for creating flexible and extensible object-oriented code in Kotlin. In the upcoming sections, we'll explore more advanced OOP topics in Kotlin, including interfaces, data classes, and sealed classes.

3.3 Interfaces and Abstract Classes

Interfaces and abstract classes are essential components of object-oriented programming in Kotlin. They provide a way to define contracts that classes must adhere to, promoting code reusability and maintainability. This section explores interfaces, abstract classes, and their usage in Kotlin.

Interfaces

An interface in Kotlin defines a contract of methods and properties that implementing classes must provide. Interfaces are defined using the `interface` keyword. Here's a simple example:

```kotlin
interface Drawable {
    fun draw()
}
```

In this example, the `Drawable` interface declares a single method `draw()`. Any class that implements this interface must provide an implementation for the `draw` method.

Implementing Interfaces

To implement an interface in Kotlin, a class uses the : `InterfaceName` syntax. Here's an example:

```kotlin
class Circle : Drawable {
    override fun draw() {
        println("Drawing a circle")
    }
}
```

In this example, the `Circle` class implements the `Drawable` interface and provides an implementation for the `draw` method.

Multiple Interfaces

A class can implement multiple interfaces in Kotlin, separating them with commas. This allows a class to adhere to multiple contracts. Here's an example:

```kotlin
interface Drawable {
    fun draw()
}

interface Clickable {
    fun onClick()
}

class Button : Drawable, Clickable {
    override fun draw() {
        println("Drawing a button")
    }

    override fun onClick() {
        println("Button clicked")
    }
}
```

In this example, the `Button` class implements both the `Drawable` and `Clickable` interfaces.

Abstract Classes

Abstract classes are similar to interfaces but can also contain abstract methods (methods without implementations). Abstract classes are defined using the `abstract` keyword. Here's an example:

```kotlin
abstract class Shape {
    abstract fun calculateArea(): Double
}
```

In this example, the `Shape` abstract class declares an abstract method `calculateArea()`. Subclasses of `Shape` must provide concrete implementations for this method.

To create a subclass of an abstract class in Kotlin, you use the : `SuperclassName()` syntax. Subclasses must provide implementations for all abstract methods declared in the superclass. Here's an example:

```
class Circle(val radius: Double) : Shape() {
    override fun calculateArea(): Double {
        return Math.PI * radius * radius
    }
}
```

In this example, the `Circle` class extends the `Shape` abstract class and provides an implementation for the `calculateArea` method.

When deciding whether to use an interface or an abstract class, consider the following:

- Use an interface when you want to define a contract that multiple classes can adhere to. Interfaces are ideal for achieving polymorphism.
- Use an abstract class when you want to provide a common base with some shared implementation (including properties and non-abstract methods) for subclasses.

Interfaces and abstract classes are powerful tools for organizing and structuring code in Kotlin. They play a crucial role in defining contracts and promoting code reuse and extensibility. In the next sections, we'll explore data classes, sealed classes, and design patterns in Kotlin.

3.4 Data Classes and Sealed Classes

Data classes and sealed classes are two specialized constructs in Kotlin that help streamline the creation and management of certain types of classes. In this section, we'll explore data classes and sealed classes and their respective use cases.

Data Classes

Data classes are designed to hold data and provide a concise way to declare classes with properties, equals(), hashCode(), and toString() methods automatically generated. To define a data class in Kotlin, you use the `data` keyword. Here's an example:

```
data class Person(val name: String, val age: Int)
```

In this example, the `Person` class is a data class with two properties: name and age. Kotlin automatically generates useful functions for data classes:

- `equals()`: Compares instances based on their properties.
- `hashCode()`: Generates a hash code based on the properties.

- `toString()`: Provides a human-readable representation of the object.

You can create instances of data classes and use their properties like regular classes:

```
val person1 = Person("Alice", 30)
val person2 = Person("Bob", 25)

println(person1) // Prints: Person(name=Alice, age=30)
println(person1 == person2) // Prints: false
```

Data classes are particularly useful for representing simple data structures and reducing boilerplate code.

Sealed Classes

Sealed classes are used to represent a restricted hierarchy of classes, where all subclasses are known and limited. They are often used in situations where you have a fixed set of possible types, such as when modeling state transitions or handling different cases in a controlled manner. To define a sealed class, use the `sealed` keyword. Here's an example:

```
sealed class Result
class Success(val data: String) : Result()
class Error(val message: String) : Result()
```

In this example, the `Result` sealed class has two subclasses: `Success` and `Error`. The sealed class restricts the set of possible subclasses.

Sealed classes are often used in conjunction with when expressions for exhaustive handling of all possible cases:

```
fun processResult(result: Result) {
    when (result) {
        is Success -> println("Success: ${result.data}")
        is Error -> println("Error: ${result.message}")
    }
}
```

Using a sealed class ensures that you handle all possible cases, and the Kotlin compiler helps you detect any missing cases.

Additional Benefits

Both data classes and sealed classes provide a level of abstraction and help improve code readability. Data classes simplify the creation and management of classes designed for data storage, while sealed classes help enforce strict hierarchies for certain types.

By using these constructs appropriately, you can make your code more concise, maintainable, and less error-prone. In the following sections, we'll delve into more advanced Kotlin concepts and design patterns for object-oriented programming.

3.5 Design Patterns in Kotlin

Design patterns are well-established solutions to common programming problems. They provide templates and best practices for structuring code to achieve specific goals. In this section, we'll explore some commonly used design patterns in Kotlin and how they can be applied to Android app development.

Singleton Pattern

The Singleton pattern ensures that a class has only one instance and provides a global point of access to it. In Kotlin, you can implement a Singleton using the `object` keyword:

```kotlin
object MySingleton {
    fun doSomething() {
        // Singleton logic here
    }
}
```

You can access the Singleton instance like this:

```kotlin
MySingleton.doSomething()
```

Singletons are useful for managing shared resources, such as database connections, logging, and configuration settings, in an Android app.

Factory Method Pattern

The Factory Method pattern defines an interface for creating objects but allows subclasses to alter the type of objects that will be created. It's helpful when you need to create objects without specifying the exact class of object that will be created. Here's a simplified example:

```kotlin
interface Product {
    fun displayInfo()
}

class ConcreteProductA : Product {
    override fun displayInfo() {
        println("Product A")
    }
}

class ConcreteProductB : Product {
    override fun displayInfo() {
        println("Product B")
    }
}
```

```kotlin
abstract class ProductFactory {
    abstract fun createProduct(): Product
}

class ConcreteProductFactoryA : ProductFactory() {
    override fun createProduct(): Product {
        return ConcreteProductA()
    }
}

class ConcreteProductFactoryB : ProductFactory() {
    override fun createProduct(): Product {
        return ConcreteProductB()
    }
}
```

In this example, we have two concrete product classes (Product A and Product B) and two concrete factory classes (Factory A and Factory B). Each factory is responsible for creating a specific product.

Observer Pattern

The Observer pattern is used for implementing distributed event handling systems. It defines a one-to-many dependency between objects so that when one object changes state, all its dependents are notified and updated automatically. In Android, this pattern is often used for implementing UI components that react to changes in underlying data.

Kotlin provides a convenient way to implement the Observer pattern using the Observable and Observer classes. Here's a simplified example:

```kotlin
import java.util.Observable
import java.util.Observer

class MyObservable : Observable() {
    fun doSomething() {
        setChanged()
        notifyObservers("Something happened")
    }
}

class MyObserver : Observer {
    override fun update(o: Observable?, arg: Any?) {
        if (o is MyObservable) {
            println("Observer received: $arg")
        }
    }
}

fun main() {
    val observable = MyObservable()
```

```kotlin
    val observer = MyObserver()

    observable.addObserver(observer)

    observable.doSomething()
}
```

In this example, `MyObservable` is the subject that notifies its observers when something happens. `MyObserver` is the observer that reacts to changes in the subject.

Builder Pattern

The Builder pattern separates the construction of a complex object from its representation. It allows you to create an object step by step, providing flexibility in the construction process. Kotlin's named parameters and default arguments make it well-suited for implementing the Builder pattern without the need for external libraries.

Here's an example:

```kotlin
class Product(
    val name: String,
    val price: Double,
    val description: String = "",
    val category: String = "General"
)

class ProductBuilder {
    var name: String = ""
    var price: Double = 0.0
    var description: String = ""
    var category: String = "General"

    fun build(): Product {
        return Product(name, price, description, category)
    }
}
```

You can create a `Product` using the `ProductBuilder` like this:

```kotlin
val product = ProductBuilder()
    .name("Widget")
    .price(19.99)
    .description("A useful widget")
    .build()
```

The Builder pattern simplifies object creation, especially for objects with many optional parameters.

These are just a few examples of design patterns that can be applied in Kotlin to improve the organization, maintainability, and flexibility of your Android app code. Understanding and utilizing design patterns can help you write more efficient and maintainable code in Android app development.

Chapter 4: Building User Interfaces with Kotlin

4.1 Introduction to Android UI Components

User interfaces are a crucial part of Android app development. Creating visually appealing and interactive user interfaces is essential for delivering a great user experience. In this section, we'll introduce you to Android UI components and the fundamental concepts of building user interfaces in Kotlin.

Android UI Hierarchy

Android user interfaces are constructed using a hierarchy of UI components known as Views. Views are the building blocks of the user interface and can represent various elements, such as buttons, text fields, images, and more. Views are organized in a tree-like structure, with a single root view at the top.

Here's an overview of the Android UI hierarchy:

- **ViewGroup**: ViewGroup is a base class for layouts. It can contain other views or view groups. Examples of ViewGroups include LinearLayout, RelativeLayout, and ConstraintLayout.

- **View**: View is the base class for all UI components. It represents a rectangular area on the screen and can respond to user input events. Examples of Views include TextView, ImageView, and Button.

- **Layouts**: Layouts are special ViewGroups used to organize the placement and arrangement of other views. They control how views are positioned and sized within the user interface. Common layouts include LinearLayout (for linear arrangement), RelativeLayout (for relative positioning), and ConstraintLayout (for complex layouts with constraints).

- **Widgets**: Widgets are interactive UI elements that the user can interact with, such as buttons, checkboxes, and text input fields.

XML Layouts

In Android, you can define the structure and appearance of your user interface using XML layout files. These layout files describe the arrangement and properties of UI components in a human-readable format. The Android system then inflates these XML layouts at runtime to create the user interface.

Here's a simple example of an XML layout file for a basic login screen:

```xml
<?xml version="1.0" encoding="utf-8"?>
<LinearLayout xmlns:android="http://schemas.android.com/apk/res/android"
    android:layout_width="match_parent"
    android:layout_height="match_parent"
```

```xml
    android:orientation="vertical"
    android:padding="16dp">

    <EditText
        android:id="@+id/editTextUsername"
        android:layout_width="match_parent"
        android:layout_height="wrap_content"
        android:hint="Username" />

    <EditText
        android:id="@+id/editTextPassword"
        android:layout_width="match_parent"
        android:layout_height="wrap_content"
        android:hint="Password"
        android:inputType="textPassword" />

    <Button
        android:id="@+id/buttonLogin"
        android:layout_width="match_parent"
        android:layout_height="wrap_content"
        android:text="Login" />
```

```xml
</LinearLayout>
```

In this XML layout, we use a `LinearLayout` to arrange two `EditText` views for username and password input and a `Button` for login. Each view has its attributes defined in XML.

Programmatically Creating Views

While XML layouts are the preferred way to define user interfaces in Android, you can also create and manipulate views programmatically in Kotlin. This is useful when you need to dynamically generate or modify views based on runtime conditions.

Here's a basic example of creating a `TextView` programmatically and adding it to a `LinearLayout`:

```kotlin
val linearLayout = findViewById<LinearLayout>(R.id.linearLayoutContainer)

val textView = TextView(this)
textView.text = "Hello, World!"
textView.layoutParams = ViewGroup.LayoutParams(
    ViewGroup.LayoutParams.WRAP_CONTENT,
    ViewGroup.LayoutParams.WRAP_CONTENT
)
```

```kotlin
linearLayout.addView(textView)
```

In this code, we create a `TextView` instance, set its text and layout parameters, and then add it to a `LinearLayout` with the specified ID.

Understanding the Android UI hierarchy, XML layouts, and programmatic view creation is essential for building user interfaces in Android using Kotlin. In the following sections, we'll delve deeper into layout design, user input handling, and creating custom views.

4.2 Layouts and Views in Android

In Android app development, layouts and views play a central role in defining the structure and appearance of user interfaces. Layouts are responsible for arranging views on the screen, while views are the individual UI components displayed to the user. This section explores the various layout types and views available in Android.

Layout Types

Android provides several layout types that determine how views are organized and positioned on the screen. Here are some common layout types:

- **LinearLayout**: LinearLayout arranges child views in a single row or column, either horizontally or vertically. You can use attributes like `android:orientation` to specify the orientation.

- **RelativeLayout**: RelativeLayout allows you to position child views relative to each other or to the parent view. You can use attributes like `android:layout_above`, `android:layout_below`, etc., to define relationships.

- **ConstraintLayout**: ConstraintLayout is a versatile layout that allows you to create complex UI designs with flexible constraints. It's particularly useful for responsive and adaptive layouts.

- **FrameLayout**: FrameLayout is a simple layout that stacks child views on top of each other. It's often used for displaying single views at a time, such as fragments.

- **GridLayout**: GridLayout arranges child views in a grid with rows and columns. It's suitable for creating grid-based layouts.

- **CoordinatorLayout**: CoordinatorLayout is a specialized layout designed for coordinating the behavior of child views, particularly in the context of Material Design and complex animations.

Views

Views are the building blocks of Android user interfaces. Android provides a wide range of pre-built views for various purposes. Some common views include:

- **TextView**: TextView is used for displaying text on the screen. You can customize its appearance, such as font size, color, and style.

- **EditText**: EditText is an input field that allows users to enter text. It's commonly used for forms and user input.

- **Button**: Button is a clickable view that triggers actions when pressed. It's used for actions like submitting forms or navigating between screens.

- **ImageView**: ImageView is used to display images. It supports various image formats, including JPEG, PNG, and GIF.

- **CheckBox**: CheckBox allows users to select multiple options from a list. It's often used in settings and preference screens.

- **RadioButton**: RadioButton is similar to a CheckBox but allows users to select a single option from a list.

- **SeekBar**: SeekBar provides a draggable slider for selecting values within a range. It's often used for settings like volume control.

- **Spinner**: Spinner is a drop-down list that allows users to select one option from a list of choices.

- **ListView**: ListView is used to display a scrollable list of items. It's commonly used for displaying lists of data.

- **RecyclerView**: RecyclerView is a more flexible and efficient version of ListView for displaying large lists of data with complex item layouts.

- **WebView**: WebView is a view that displays web content, such as web pages or HTML documents, within an Android app.

These are just a few examples of the many views available in Android. Views can be customized and combined to create rich and interactive user interfaces.

XML Layouts for Views

To define the arrangement and properties of views in Android, XML layout files are commonly used. In XML layouts, you specify the type of layout and views, their attributes, and their relationships within the layout hierarchy.

Here's a simple example of an XML layout that uses a RelativeLayout to arrange a TextView and a Button:

```xml
<?xml version="1.0" encoding="utf-8"?>
<RelativeLayout xmlns:android="http://schemas.android.com/apk/res/android"
    android:layout_width="match_parent"
    android:layout_height="match_parent">

    <TextView
        android:id="@+id/textViewMessage"
        android:layout_width="wrap_content"
        android:layout_height="wrap_content"
        android:text="Hello, Android!"
        android:layout_centerInParent="true" />
```

```
<Button
    android:id="@+id/buttonClickMe"
    android:layout_width="wrap_content"
    android:layout_height="wrap_content"
    android:text="Click Me"
    android:layout_below="@+id/textViewMessage"
    android:layout_centerHorizontal="true" />
```

```
</RelativeLayout>
```

In this layout, the TextView is centered in the parent RelativeLayout, and the Button is positioned below the TextView and centered horizontally. These layout attributes help define the structure of the user interface.

Understanding the different layout types and views available in Android is essential for designing user-friendly and responsive app interfaces. In the next sections, we'll explore user input handling, custom views, and advanced UI components in Android app development.

4.3 User Input Handling

User input handling is a fundamental aspect of Android app development. Apps often require users to interact with the interface by tapping buttons, entering text, making selections, and more. In this section, we'll explore how to handle user input in Android using Kotlin.

Event Handling

In Android, user interactions generate events, such as button clicks, text input, and touch gestures. To respond to these events, you can use event listeners or event handling methods. Here are some common ways to handle user input events:

- **OnClickListener**: This listener is used to handle click events on views like buttons. You can set an OnClickListener to a view and define the action to be taken when the view is clicked.

```
val button = findViewById<Button>(R.id.myButton)
button.setOnClickListener {
    // Handle button click here
}
```

- **TextWatcher**: TextWatcher is used to monitor changes in EditText fields. It provides methods like beforeTextChanged, onTextChanged, and afterTextChanged to react to text changes.

```
val editText = findViewById<EditText>(R.id.myEditText)
editText.addTextChangedListener(object : TextWatcher {
```

```kotlin
    override fun beforeTextChanged(s: CharSequence?, start: Int, count:
Int, after: Int) {
        // Called before text changes
    }

    override fun onTextChanged(s: CharSequence?, start: Int, before: In
t, count: Int) {
        // Called during text changes
    }

    override fun afterTextChanged(s: Editable?) {
        // Called after text changes
    }
})
```

- **OnItemSelectedListener**: This listener is used with Spinner widgets to detect item selections.

```kotlin
val spinner = findViewById<Spinner>(R.id.mySpinner)
spinner.onItemSelectedListener = object : AdapterView.OnItemSelectedLis
tener {
    override fun onItemSelected(parent: AdapterView<*>?, view: View?, p
osition: Int, id: Long) {
        // Handle item selection
    }

    override fun onNothingSelected(parent: AdapterView<*>?) {
        // Handle nothing selected
    }
}
```

- **GestureDetector**: GestureDetector is used to detect touch gestures like taps, swipes, and scrolls.

```kotlin
val gestureDetector = GestureDetector(this, object : GestureDetector.Si
mpleOnGestureListener() {
    override fun onSingleTapUp(e: MotionEvent?): Boolean {
        // Handle single tap
        return super.onSingleTapUp(e)
    }

    override fun onFling(e1: MotionEvent?, e2: MotionEvent?, velocityX:
Float, velocityY: Float): Boolean {
        // Handle fling gesture
        return super.onFling(e1, e2, velocityX, velocityY)
    }
})

// Attach the gesture detector to a view
val myView = findViewById<View>(R.id.myView)
```

```kotlin
myView.setOnTouchListener { _, event -> gestureDetector.onTouchEvent(ev
ent) }
```

Handling User Input Validation

When handling user input, it's important to validate the data to ensure it meets the
expected criteria. For example, you may want to check if an email address is in a valid
format or if a password meets security requirements.

```kotlin
val emailEditText = findViewById<EditText>(R.id.emailEditText)
val passwordEditText = findViewById<EditText>(R.id.passwordEditText)

val email = emailEditText.text.toString()
val password = passwordEditText.text.toString()

if (!isValidEmail(email)) {
    // Display an error message for an invalid email
    emailEditText.error = "Invalid email address"
} else if (!isValidPassword(password)) {
    // Display an error message for an invalid password
    passwordEditText.error = "Password must be at least 8 characters long"
} else {
    // Input is valid, proceed with the operation
}
```

Input Methods and Soft Keyboard

Handling user input often involves managing the soft keyboard (virtual keyboard) that
appears when users interact with text fields. You can control the keyboard's behavior, such
as showing or hiding it, programmatically.

To show the soft keyboard:

```kotlin
val editText = findViewById<EditText>(R.id.myEditText)
val inputMethodManager = getSystemService(Context.INPUT_METHOD_SERVICE) as In
putMethodManager
inputMethodManager.showSoftInput(editText, InputMethodManager.SHOW_IMPLICIT)
```

To hide the soft keyboard:

```kotlin
val editText = findViewById<EditText>(R.id.myEditText)
val inputMethodManager = getSystemService(Context.INPUT_METHOD_SERVICE) as In
putMethodManager
inputMethodManager.hideSoftInputFromWindow(editText.windowToken, 0)
```

Handling user input effectively and providing appropriate feedback and validation are
essential for creating a smooth and user-friendly Android app. By understanding how to
work with input events, you can create interactive and responsive applications.

4.4 Fragments and Navigation

Fragments are a crucial part of Android app development, allowing you to create modular and reusable components for your user interface. In this section, we'll explore the concept of fragments and how they are used for building flexible and navigable user interfaces in Android. We'll also discuss navigation principles and tools for moving between different parts of your app.

Fragments in Android

A fragment is a self-contained, reusable component that represents a portion of a user interface. Fragments are often used to build multi-pane user interfaces for larger screens, such as tablets, but they are valuable in various contexts.

Fragment Lifecycle

Fragments have their own lifecycle, similar to activities. The key lifecycle methods for fragments include onCreate, onCreateView, onPause, onResume, and onDestroy, among others. You can override these methods to perform actions at specific points in a fragment's lifecycle.

Here's an example of a simple fragment:

```
class MyFragment : Fragment() {
    override fun onCreateView(
        inflater: LayoutInflater, container: ViewGroup?,
        savedInstanceState: Bundle?
    ): View? {
        // Inflate the fragment's layout
        return inflater.inflate(R.layout.fragment_my, container, false)
    }
}
```

In this example, the onCreateView method inflates a layout for the fragment. This layout defines the UI for the fragment.

Fragment Transactions

Fragments are typically added to an activity using fragment transactions. Fragment transactions are a way to add, replace, or remove fragments within an activity. You can perform fragment transactions programmatically to change the UI dynamically.

Here's an example of adding a fragment to an activity:

```
val fragmentTransaction = supportFragmentManager.beginTransaction()
val fragment = MyFragment()
fragmentTransaction.add(R.id.fragment_container, fragment)
fragmentTransaction.commit()
```

In this code, we create a fragment transaction, add an instance of `MyFragment` to the activity's layout with the ID `fragment_container`, and then commit the transaction.

Navigation in Android

Navigation is the process of moving between different parts of an app's user interface. In Android, navigation can involve transitioning between activities, fragments, or views. Effective navigation is crucial for providing a seamless user experience.

Navigation Components

Android Jetpack includes the Navigation component, which simplifies navigation and helps you implement best practices for app navigation. The Navigation component provides tools for defining the navigation flow of your app, managing navigation destinations, and handling the back stack.

With Navigation component, you can define navigation graphs that represent the possible paths users can take through your app. You can also use safe arguments to pass data between destinations.

Navigating to Fragments

To navigate to a fragment using the Navigation component, you typically define actions in your navigation graph that specify the source and destination fragments. Then, you use the `NavController` to navigate between them.

Here's an example of navigating to a fragment:

```
val action = MyFragmentDirections.actionMyFragmentToAnotherFragment()
findNavController().navigate(action)
```

In this code, `actionMyFragmentToAnotherFragment` is an automatically generated action defined in the navigation graph. It specifies the navigation from `MyFragment` to another fragment.

Back Stack and Up Navigation

The Navigation component also handles the back stack, allowing users to navigate backward through the app's navigation hierarchy. You can use the `popBackStack` method to navigate back to the previous destination.

Additionally, the Navigation component provides built-in support for up navigation, which allows users to navigate up through the app's hierarchy to a parent screen. You can define parent destinations in your navigation graph to enable up navigation.

Effective use of fragments and navigation principles is essential for building intuitive and well-structured Android apps. Fragments provide a modular approach to building user interfaces, and the Navigation component simplifies the implementation of navigation flows, ensuring a smooth user experience.

4.5 Custom Views and ViewGroups

While Android provides a wide range of built-in views and viewgroups for creating user interfaces, there are situations where you may need to create custom views and viewgroups tailored to your app's specific requirements. In this section, we'll explore how to create custom views and viewgroups in Android using Kotlin.

Custom Views

Custom views allow you to create unique UI components that are not available as standard views. You can define custom views by extending the `View` class or its subclasses, such as `TextView` or `ImageView`. Here's an example of a custom view that displays a colored circle:

```kotlin
class CircleView(context: Context, attrs: AttributeSet) : View(context, attrs
) {
    private val paint = Paint(Paint.ANTI_ALIAS_FLAG)
    private var circleColor: Int = Color.BLUE

    init {
        // Initialize paint properties
        paint.style = Paint.Style.FILL
        paint.color = circleColor
    }

    override fun onDraw(canvas: Canvas?) {
        super.onDraw(canvas)

        // Get the view's dimensions
        val width = width.toFloat()
        val height = height.toFloat()

        // Calculate the radius as half of the smaller dimension
        val radius = if (width < height) width / 2 else height / 2

        // Calculate the center of the view
        val centerX = width / 2
        val centerY = height / 2

        // Draw the circle
        canvas?.drawCircle(centerX, centerY, radius, paint)
    }

    fun setCircleColor(color: Int) {
        circleColor = color
        paint.color = circleColor
        // Invalidate the view to trigger a redraw
        invalidate()
```

```
        }
}
```

In this example, the CircleView class extends View and overrides the onDraw method to draw a colored circle. You can customize the circle's color by calling the setCircleColor method.

Custom ViewGroups

Custom viewgroups are used to create custom layouts or containers for arranging child views. You can define custom viewgroups by extending the ViewGroup class or one of its subclasses, such as LinearLayout or RelativeLayout. Here's an example of a custom FlowLayout viewgroup that arranges child views in a flow layout:

```
class FlowLayout(context: Context, attrs: AttributeSet) : ViewGroup(context,
attrs) {

    override fun onMeasure(widthMeasureSpec: Int, heightMeasureSpec: Int) {
        // Measure child views and calculate the size of this viewgroup
        // ...
    }

    override fun onLayout(changed: Boolean, l: Int, t: Int, r: Int, b: Int) {
        // Position child views within this viewgroup
        // ...
    }
}
```

In this example, the FlowLayout class extends ViewGroup and overrides the onMeasure and onLayout methods to define the layout behavior.

Using Custom Views and ViewGroups

To use custom views and viewgroups in your layout XML files, you need to fully qualify their class names with the package name, and you can pass attributes as necessary. For example:

```
<com.example.myapp.CircleView
    android:layout_width="100dp"
    android:layout_height="100dp"
    app:circleColor="#FF5722" />
```

In this XML layout, a CircleView is used with a custom attribute app:circleColor to set the circle's color.

Custom views and viewgroups provide flexibility in designing your app's user interface. They allow you to create UI components that perfectly match your app's design and functionality requirements. Understanding how to create and use custom views and viewgroups can significantly enhance your Android app development capabilities.

Chapter 5: Working with Android Resources

5.1 Understanding Android Resource System

Android apps often need to access various types of resources, such as strings, images, layouts, and more, to provide a rich user experience. In this section, we'll delve into the Android resource system, which allows you to manage and use these resources efficiently in your Kotlin-based Android applications.

What Are Android Resources?

Android resources are external assets and data files that are separate from your app's source code. Resources include:

- **Strings**: Text and string values used in your app, such as labels, messages, and prompts.

- **Drawables**: Images, icons, and graphics that are part of your app's user interface.

- **Layouts**: XML files that define the structure and arrangement of user interface components.

- **Colors**: Color definitions used throughout your app's design.

- **Dimensions**: Measurement values, such as sizes and margins, used for layout and design.

- **Animations**: Animation resources that define how views should animate.

- **Raw Files**: Arbitrary files, such as audio, video, or JSON data, that can be accessed as resources.

Resource Folders and Qualifiers

Android organizes resources into different folders based on qualifiers. Qualifiers specify characteristics like screen size, orientation, and language. This allows Android to select the appropriate resource version for the current device configuration automatically.

Here are some common resource qualifiers:

- **Drawable Resources**: Drawable resources are organized into folders with qualifiers like mdpi, hdpi, xhdpi, xxhdpi, and xxxhdpi to support different screen densities.

- **Layout Resources**: Layout resources can be placed in folders with qualifiers like layout, layout-land (for landscape orientation), and layout-sw600dp (for a screen width of at least 600dp).

- **String Resources**: String resources are stored in `res/values` folders, and different versions can be created for different languages using qualifiers like `values-en` or `values-fr`.

To access resources in your Kotlin code, you can use the `R` class, which is generated by the Android build process. The `R` class contains static nested classes for various types of resources.

For example, to access a string resource, you can use the following code:

```
val appName = getString(R.string.app_name)
```

Here, `R.string.app_name` refers to the string resource defined in your app's `res/values/strings.xml` file.

Android allows you to provide resources for different languages and regions, ensuring your app can be used by a global audience. When a user's device is set to a specific language, Android automatically selects the appropriate resources.

To support multiple languages, you can create resource files with different qualifiers. For example, to provide Spanish translations, you can create a `values-es` folder and place string resources with Spanish translations there.

```
<!-- res/values-es/strings.xml -->
<resources>
    <string name="app_name">Mi Aplicación</string>
</resources>
```

Android will automatically switch to the Spanish version of the resource when the user's device language is set to Spanish.

Understanding the Android resource system is essential for building apps that are easily maintainable, scalable, and adaptable to different devices and languages. Proper resource management ensures your app provides a consistent and localized user experience.

5.2 Handling Strings and Localization

String resources are a fundamental part of Android app development. They allow you to separate text and labels from your code, making it easier to translate your app into different languages and maintain a consistent user experience. In this section, we'll explore how to work with string resources and implement localization in Android using Kotlin.

String Resource Definition

String resources are defined in XML files located in the `res/values` folder of your Android project. By using string resources, you can reference text throughout your app's user interface and code, making it more accessible for localization and updates.

Here's an example of defining string resources in `res/values/strings.xml`:

```xml
<resources>
    <string name="app_name">MyApp</string>
    <string name="welcome_message">Welcome to MyApp!</string>
    <string name="button_label">Click Me</string>
</resources>
```

In this XML file, we've defined three string resources: `app_name`, `welcome_message`, and `button_label`.

Accessing String Resources

To access string resources in your Kotlin code, you can use the `getString` method, passing the resource's identifier (usually `R.string.resource_name`). Here's an example:

```kotlin
val appName = getString(R.string.app_name)
val welcomeMessage = getString(R.string.welcome_message)
val buttonLabel = getString(R.string.button_label)
```

By using string resources in your code, you can easily change text across your app by updating the corresponding resource values without modifying code.

Localization

Localization is the process of adapting your app for different languages and regions. Android provides robust support for localization through resource qualifiers.

For instance, to provide translations for Spanish, you can create a `values-es` folder and place a `strings.xml` file with translated strings. Here's an example:

```xml
<!-- res/values-es/strings.xml -->
<resources>
    <string name="app_name">MiAplicación</string>
    <string name="welcome_message">¡Bienvenido a MiAplicación!</string>
    <string name="button_label">Haz clic</string>
</resources>
```

Android will automatically select the appropriate resources based on the device's language settings. If the device is set to Spanish, it will use the translations from `values-es`.

Providing Multiple Resource Qualifiers

You can provide different resource qualifiers for various device configurations, such as screen size, orientation, and more. For example, you can create `values-large` or `values-sw600dp` folders to specify resources for devices with larger screens.

To test different device configurations, you can use the Android Virtual Device (AVD) manager to create virtual devices with various characteristics.

String Formatting

In addition to simple strings, you can use string resources for formatted text. Android supports string formatting using placeholders. For example:

```
<string name="welcome_message">Welcome, %s!</string>
```

In code, you can use `getString` with arguments to replace placeholders:

```
val username = "John"
val welcomeMessage = getString(R.string.welcome_message, username)
```

This allows you to create dynamic and context-aware strings.

Properly managing string resources and implementing localization are essential for making your Android app accessible to a global audience. By separating text from code and providing translations, you can ensure a user-friendly experience for users worldwide.

5.3 Managing Images and Drawables

Images and drawables are crucial for creating visually appealing Android apps. In this section, we'll explore how to manage images and drawables in Android using Kotlin. We'll cover different types of drawables, ways to display images, and best practices for handling visual assets.

Types of Drawables

Android supports various types of drawables, each suitable for specific use cases:

1. **Bitmap Drawables**: These are images in formats like PNG, JPEG, and GIF. Bitmap drawables are the most common and versatile type of drawables used for images and icons.

2. **Vector Drawables**: Vector drawables are defined using XML and can be scaled without loss of quality. They are ideal for icons and graphics that need to adapt to different screen sizes and resolutions.

3. **Nine-Patch Drawables**: Nine-patch drawables are specialized bitmaps that allow you to define stretchable areas. They are often used for creating resizable backgrounds and buttons.

4. **Layer Drawables**: Layer drawables combine multiple drawables into a single drawable, allowing you to create complex visuals by layering different elements.

Placing Drawables in Resources

Just like string resources, drawables are placed in resource folders. Common resource folders for drawables include:

- `res/drawable-mdpi`: For medium-density screens.
- `res/drawable-hdpi`: For high-density screens.
- `res/drawable-xhdpi`: For extra-high-density screens.
- `res/drawable-xxhdpi`: For extra-extra-high-density screens.
- `res/drawable-xxxhdpi`: For extra-extra-extra-high-density screens.

You can create drawable resources by copying image files into the appropriate folders or by creating vector drawables using XML.

Displaying Images in XML Layouts

To display images in XML layouts, you can use the `ImageView` widget. Here's an example of how to display an image in an XML layout:

```
<ImageView
    android:id="@+id/myImageView"
    android:layout_width="wrap_content"
    android:layout_height="wrap_content"
    android:src="@drawable/my_image" />
```

In this example, `my_image` refers to the drawable resource you want to display. You can customize the layout dimensions and other attributes as needed.

Displaying Images Programmatically

In Kotlin code, you can reference and display drawables using the `ImageView` widget and the `setImageResource` method. Here's an example:

```
val imageView = findViewById<ImageView>(R.id.myImageView)
imageView.setImageResource(R.drawable.my_image)
```

You can also create drawable objects programmatically and set them to an `ImageView`:

```
val drawable = ResourcesCompat.getDrawable(resources, R.drawable.my_image, null)
imageView.setImageDrawable(drawable)
```

Supporting Multiple Screen Densities

To provide images for different screen densities, you should create multiple versions of your drawables and place them in the appropriate density-specific folders. Android will automatically select the correct drawable based on the device's screen density.

It's important to follow best practices for image asset creation and optimization to ensure that your app performs well and looks great on various devices. Properly managing drawables is essential for delivering a visually appealing and responsive user experience in your Android app.

5.4 Using XML Layout Resources

XML layout resources are a fundamental part of Android app development. They define the structure and arrangement of user interface components, allowing you to create responsive and visually appealing app layouts. In this section, we'll dive into using XML layout resources in Android with Kotlin.

Anatomy of an XML Layout

An XML layout file represents the structure of a screen or a part of a screen in your Android app. It typically consists of the following elements:

1. **Root Element**: The root element of an XML layout defines the type of layout used (e.g., LinearLayout, RelativeLayout, ConstraintLayout, etc.).

2. **View Elements**: View elements represent UI components like buttons, text views, image views, and more. They are defined within the root element and include attributes that specify their properties.

3. **Attributes**: Attributes are used to configure the properties of view elements, such as dimensions, margins, padding, text, and appearance.

Here's a simple example of an XML layout for a button:

```
<RelativeLayout xmlns:android="http://schemas.android.com/apk/res/android"
    android:layout_width="match_parent"
    android:layout_height="match_parent">

    <Button
        android:id="@+id/myButton"
        android:layout_width="wrap_content"
        android:layout_height="wrap_content"
        android:text="Click Me" />
</RelativeLayout>
```

In this XML layout, we have a RelativeLayout as the root element containing a Button with attributes specifying its ID, dimensions, and text.

Referencing XML Layouts

To use an XML layout in your Kotlin code, you can inflate it using the LayoutInflater and attach it to an activity or fragment. Here's an example:

```
val inflater = LayoutInflater.from(this)
val layout = inflater.inflate(R.layout.my_layout, null)
```

In this code, R.layout.my_layout refers to the XML layout resource you want to inflate. You can then add the layout view to your activity's or fragment's view hierarchy as needed.

Accessing Views in XML Layouts

To interact with views defined in XML layouts, you can find and reference them in your Kotlin code using their IDs. Here's an example of how to access a button defined in an XML layout:

```
val button = findViewById<Button>(R.id.myButton)
button.setOnClickListener {
    // Handle button click event
}
```

By referencing views in this way, you can manipulate their properties and respond to user interactions programmatically.

Layout Variants and Resource Qualifiers

To create responsive layouts for different screen sizes and orientations, you can define layout variants using resource qualifiers. For example, you can create a layout folder for the default layout, a layout-land folder for landscape layouts, and specific folders for different screen sizes (layout-sw600dp for larger screens, etc.). Android will automatically select the appropriate layout based on the device's characteristics.

XML layout resources are a powerful tool for designing flexible and adaptive user interfaces in Android apps. They allow you to separate the visual structure from the code logic, making it easier to maintain and scale your app's user interface. Properly leveraging XML layouts is essential for delivering a great user experience on diverse Android devices.

5.5 Styles and Themes in Android

Styles and themes are important aspects of Android app development that allow you to define consistent visual elements, such as colors, fonts, and layouts, across your app. In this section, we'll explore how to use styles and themes in Android apps developed with Kotlin.

Styles vs. Themes

Styles and **themes** are related but serve slightly different purposes:

- **Styles**: A style is a collection of attributes that define the appearance and behavior of a view or a group of views. Styles are defined in XML files and can be applied to individual view elements in your layout XML or programmatically in Kotlin code.

- **Themes**: A theme is a set of styles that define the overall look and feel of your app. Themes are defined in XML files and applied at the application or activity level. They provide a consistent visual identity to your app, affecting elements like the app's toolbar, text color, and more.

Defining Styles

Styles are typically defined in XML files, often located in the `res/values` folder. Here's an example of defining a style in `res/values/styles.xml`:

```
<style name="MyButtonStyle">
    <item name="android:layout_width">wrap_content</item>
    <item name="android:layout_height">wrap_content</item>
    <item name="android:textSize">16sp</item>
    <item name="android:padding">8dp</item>
</style>
```

In this example, we've defined a style called `MyButtonStyle` with attributes like `layout_width`, `layout_height`, `textSize`, and `padding`.

Applying Styles

You can apply a style to a view element in your layout XML by using the `style` attribute. For example, to apply the `MyButtonStyle` to a `Button`, you can do the following:

```
<Button
    android:id="@+id/myButton"
    style="@style/MyButtonStyle"
    android:text="Click Me" />
```

Alternatively, you can apply a style programmatically in Kotlin code using the `R.style` reference:

```
val button = findViewById<Button>(R.id.myButton)
button.setStyle(R.style.MyButtonStyle)
```

Defining Themes

Themes are defined in XML files, usually located in the `res/values` folder. An app can have multiple themes for different purposes, such as a light theme, a dark theme, or a theme for specific device configurations. Here's an example of defining a theme in `res/values/themes.xml`:

```
<style name="AppTheme" parent="Theme.AppCompat.Light.DarkActionBar">
    <item name="colorPrimary">@color/colorPrimary</item>
    <item name="colorPrimaryDark">@color/colorPrimaryDark</item>
    <item name="colorAccent">@color/colorAccent</item>
</style>
```

In this example, we've defined an `AppTheme` that inherits from `Theme.AppCompat.Light.DarkActionBar` and sets primary, primary dark, and accent colors.

Applying Themes

You can apply a theme to your app in the `AndroidManifest.xml` file by specifying it as the `android:theme` attribute for the `<application>` or `<activity>` element:

```
<application
    android:theme="@style/AppTheme"
    ...
</application>
```

Alternatively, you can set the theme for an activity in the `AndroidManifest.xml`:

```
<activity
    android:name=".MainActivity"
    android:theme="@style/AppTheme"
    ...
</activity>
```

Customizing Themes

Themes can be customized to change the appearance of various UI elements. You can customize themes further by creating custom styles and applying them within the theme.

Styles and themes are essential for achieving a consistent and visually appealing design in your Android app. They help you maintain a unified look and feel across different parts of your application and make it easier to adapt to different screen sizes and orientations. Properly defining and applying styles and themes is a key aspect of Android app development.

Chapter 6: Building Interactive Apps

6.1 Event Handling and Click Listeners

Event handling is a crucial aspect of Android app development that allows you to respond to user interactions, such as button clicks, touch events, and gestures. In this section, we'll explore the basics of event handling and how to use click listeners to handle user clicks on various UI elements.

Understanding Event Handling

Event handling in Android revolves around the concept of listeners. A listener is an interface or callback that waits for a specific event to occur and then executes a predefined action in response to that event. Common events in Android include button clicks, touch events, key presses, and more.

Implementing Click Listeners

Click listeners are used to handle button clicks and other similar user interactions. Here's how you can implement a click listener for a button in Kotlin:

```kotlin
val myButton = findViewById<Button>(R.id.myButton)

myButton.setOnClickListener {
    // Code to be executed when the button is clicked
    Toast.makeText(this, "Button Clicked!", Toast.LENGTH_SHORT).show()
}
```

In this example, we first obtain a reference to the button with the ID myButton. We then use the setOnClickListener function to attach a click listener to the button. Inside the listener block, we define the code that should run when the button is clicked, which in this case displays a toast message.

Using Anonymous Inner Classes

You can also implement click listeners using anonymous inner classes in Kotlin. Here's an example:

```kotlin
val anotherButton = findViewById<Button>(R.id.anotherButton)

anotherButton.setOnClickListener(object : View.OnClickListener {
    override fun onClick(v: View?) {
        // Code to be executed when the button is clicked
        Toast.makeText(this@YourActivity, "Another Button Clicked!", Toast.LENGTH_SHORT).show()
    }
})
```

In this example, we create an anonymous inner class that implements the `View.OnClickListener` interface. Inside the `onClick` method, we specify the code to run when the button is clicked.

Click Listeners for Other Views

Click listeners can be applied to various UI elements, not just buttons. For example, you can use click listeners with image views, text views, or any other clickable view elements. The process is the same: obtain a reference to the view and attach a click listener.

```
val imageView = findViewById<ImageView>(R.id.imageView)

imageView.setOnClickListener {
    // Code to be executed when the image view is clicked
    // Perform image-related actions here
}
```

Event Handling Best Practices

When implementing event handling in your Android app, consider the following best practices:

- Keep event handling code concise and focused on the specific action you want to perform in response to the event.
- Avoid blocking the main UI thread with time-consuming tasks; use background threads or coroutines for such tasks.
- Ensure that you handle exceptions gracefully to prevent crashes or unexpected behavior.
- Test your event handling thoroughly on different devices and screen sizes to ensure a consistent user experience.

Event handling and click listeners are fundamental concepts for building interactive Android apps. By understanding how to handle user interactions effectively, you can create responsive and user-friendly applications that meet your users' expectations.

6.2 Gestures and Touch Events

In addition to basic click events, Android provides support for more complex user interactions through gestures and touch events. Gestures enable you to recognize and respond to actions like swipes, pinches, and rotations, enhancing the interactivity and user experience of your app. In this section, we'll explore how to work with gestures and touch events in Android.

Gesture Detection

Android offers a built-in `GestureDetector` class that simplifies the detection of common gestures. You can use this class to recognize gestures like single taps, double taps, long presses, swipes, and more.

Here's an example of setting up a `GestureDetector` to detect a simple single tap gesture in an activity:

```
class MyActivity : AppCompatActivity() {
    private lateinit var gestureDetector: GestureDetectorCompat

    override fun onCreate(savedInstanceState: Bundle?) {
        super.onCreate(savedInstanceState)
        setContentView(R.layout.activity_my)

        gestureDetector = GestureDetectorCompat(this, object : GestureDetecto
r.SimpleOnGestureListener() {
            override fun onSingleTapConfirmed(e: MotionEvent): Boolean {
                // Handle the single tap gesture here
                return true
            }
        })
    }

    override fun onTouchEvent(event: MotionEvent): Boolean {
        return gestureDetector.onTouchEvent(event)
    }
}
```

In this example, we create a `GestureDetector` instance and override the `onSingleTapConfirmed` method to handle the single tap gesture. We then attach the `GestureDetector` to the `onTouchEvent` method of the activity to process touch events.

Custom Gesture Detection

For more advanced gesture recognition or custom gestures, you can implement your own gesture detection logic by extending the `GestureDetector.SimpleOnGestureListener` class. This allows you to define custom gestures and their associated actions.

Here's a simplified example of custom gesture detection for a swipe gesture:

```
class MyActivity : AppCompatActivity() {
    private lateinit var gestureDetector: GestureDetectorCompat

    override fun onCreate(savedInstanceState: Bundle?) {
        super.onCreate(savedInstanceState)
        setContentView(R.layout.activity_my)

        gestureDetector = GestureDetectorCompat(this, MyGestureListener())
```

```kotlin
    }

    override fun onTouchEvent(event: MotionEvent): Boolean {
        return gestureDetector.onTouchEvent(event)
    }

    inner class MyGestureListener : GestureDetector.SimpleOnGestureListener()
{
        override fun onFling(
            e1: MotionEvent?,
            e2: MotionEvent?,
            velocityX: Float,
            velocityY: Float
        ): Boolean {
            // Handle the swipe gesture here
            if (e1 != null && e2 != null) {
                val deltaX = e2.x - e1.x
                val deltaY = e2.y - e1.y

                if (abs(deltaX) > abs(deltaY)) {
                    if (deltaX > 0) {
                        // Right swipe
                    } else {
                        // Left swipe
                    }
                } else {
                    if (deltaY > 0) {
                        // Down swipe
                    } else {
                        // Up swipe
                    }
                }
            }
            return true
        }
    }
}
```

In this custom gesture detection example, we handle the onFling method to detect swipe gestures and determine the direction of the swipe (right, left, up, or down).

Multi-Touch Events

Android also supports multi-touch events, allowing you to handle multiple touch points simultaneously. This is useful for applications like games and drawing apps where users may interact with multiple objects on the screen.

To work with multi-touch events, you can override the onTouchEvent method and use the MotionEvent object to access information about multiple touch points.

```
override fun onTouchEvent(event: MotionEvent): Boolean {
    val pointerCount = event.pointerCount
    for (i in 0 until pointerCount) {
        val x = event.getX(i)
        val y = event.getY(i)

        // Handle touch events for each pointer (finger)
    }
    return true
}
```

In this code snippet, we iterate through the touch points using the `pointerCount` property of the `MotionEvent` object and retrieve the X and Y coordinates of each touch point.

Gesture and Touch Event Best Practices

When working with gestures and touch events in Android, consider the following best practices:

- Provide feedback to the user when a gesture is recognized, such as visual cues or animations.
- Ensure that gesture handling does not interfere with basic touch events like scrolling or clicking.
- Test your gesture detection on various device screen sizes and resolutions to ensure accuracy.
- Keep gesture handling code organized and modular to make it easier to maintain and debug.

Gestures and touch events add interactivity and responsiveness to your Android apps, making them more engaging for users. By implementing gesture detection and custom touch event handling, you can create rich and interactive user experiences.

6.3 Animations and Transitions

Animations and transitions are essential components of modern Android app design. They enhance the user experience by adding visual effects that provide context, feedback, and a sense of continuity. In this section, we'll explore how to implement animations and transitions in your Android app.

Property Animations

Property animations allow you to animate the properties of UI elements, such as position, size, rotation, and alpha (transparency). The Android framework provides the `ObjectAnimator` class to create property animations.

Here's an example of scaling an ImageView using property animations:

```
val imageView = findViewById<ImageView>(R.id.imageView)
val scaleUp = ObjectAnimator.ofFloat(imageView, "scaleX", 1.0f, 1.5f)
scaleUp.duration = 1000 // Animation duration in milliseconds

scaleUp.start() // Start the animation
```

In this code snippet, we create an `ObjectAnimator` that scales up the X-axis of the `imageView`. We specify the start and end values for the property, set the animation duration, and then start the animation.

ViewPropertyAnimator

The `ViewPropertyAnimator` class provides a more concise way to animate view properties. It is available directly on `View` objects and allows you to chain multiple animations together.

Here's an example of scaling and translating a View using `ViewPropertyAnimator`:

```
val myView = findViewById<View>(R.id.myView)

myView.animate()
    .scaleX(1.5f)
    .translationX(100f)
    .setDuration(1000)
    .start()
```

In this code, we call `animate()` on the `myView` and chain animations for scaling and translating. The `setDuration` method specifies the animation duration in milliseconds, and `start()` begins the animation.

Transition Animations

Transition animations are used to create smooth transitions between scenes or states in your app. Android provides the `Transition` framework to create and manage these animations.

Here's an example of a simple fade transition between two `View` elements:

```
val button1 = findViewById<Button>(R.id.button1)
val button2 = findViewById<Button>(R.id.button2)

val transition = Fade()

button1.setOnClickListener {
    val transitionManager = TransitionManager()
    transitionManager.transitionTo(Scene(rootLayout, button2))
}
```

In this code, we create a `Fade` transition and specify that we want to transition between the current view hierarchy and a new `Scene` containing `button2`. When the first button is clicked, the transition smoothly fades from the current view to the new view.

Shared Element Transitions

Shared element transitions are a type of transition animation used when transitioning between activities or fragments. They create the illusion that a specific view element transitions smoothly from one screen to another.

To implement shared element transitions, you need to specify shared elements in both the source and destination layouts, and then request the transition in your code.

```
// In the source activity or fragment
val sharedView = findViewById<View>(R.id.sharedElement)
val transitionName = "shared_element_transition"

ViewCompat.setTransitionName(sharedView, transitionName)

// In the code to start the transition to the destination activity or fragmen
t
val intent = Intent(this, DestinationActivity::class.java)
val options = ActivityOptionsCompat.makeSceneTransitionAnimation(this, shared
View, transitionName)
startActivity(intent, options.toBundle())
```

In this example, we set a transition name for the shared element using `ViewCompat.setTransitionName()`. Then, when starting the destination activity, we use `ActivityOptionsCompat.makeSceneTransitionAnimation()` to create an animation that includes the shared element.

Animation Best Practices

When implementing animations and transitions in your Android app, consider the following best practices:

- Keep animations subtle and consistent with your app's design language to avoid distracting the user.
- Test animations on different devices and screen sizes to ensure they perform smoothly.
- Use animation callbacks to coordinate other actions with the animation's timing.
- Be mindful of performance; complex animations can affect app performance, so use hardware-accelerated animations when possible.

Animations and transitions can significantly enhance the user experience in your Android app by providing visual cues and feedback. By mastering animation techniques, you can create engaging and polished applications.

6.4 Multimedia in Android

Multimedia elements, such as audio and video, are commonly integrated into Android applications to provide a richer and more engaging user experience. In this section, we'll explore how to work with multimedia in Android, including playing audio and video content.

Playing Audio

Using MediaPlayer

The MediaPlayer class in Android allows you to play audio from various sources, including local files, online streams, and resources. Here's a basic example of how to use MediaPlayer to play an audio file:

```
val mediaPlayer = MediaPlayer.create(this, R.raw.my_audio_file)
mediaPlayer.start() // Start playback
```

In this code, we create a MediaPlayer instance using MediaPlayer.create() and provide the context and resource ID of the audio file to play. We then call start() to begin audio playback.

Managing Audio Lifecycle

When working with audio playback, it's important to manage the audio lifecycle to ensure proper handling of resources and user interactions. For example, you should release the MediaPlayer when it's no longer needed and pause or stop playback when the app goes into the background.

```
override fun onPause() {
    super.onPause()
    mediaPlayer.pause() // Pause playback when the app goes into the background
}

override fun onStop() {
    super.onStop()
    mediaPlayer.release() // Release the MediaPlayer when it's no longer needed
}
```

Playing Video

Using VideoView

The VideoView widget simplifies the integration of video playback in Android apps. You can add a VideoView to your layout XML file and set its video source programmatically.

Here's an example of how to use `VideoView` to play a video from a local resource:

```
<VideoView
    android:id="@+id/videoView"
    android:layout_width="match_parent"
    android:layout_height="match_parent" />
```

```
val videoView = findViewById<VideoView>(R.id.videoView)
videoView.setVideoPath("android.resource://${packageName}/${R.raw.my_video_fi
le}")
videoView.start() // Start video playback
```

In this example, we define a `VideoView` in the layout XML and then use `setVideoPath()` to specify the video's source by providing a URI. The URI is constructed using the `android.resource://` scheme and the resource ID of the video file. Finally, we call `start()` to begin video playback.

Handling Video Events

You can register listeners to handle various video playback events, such as completion or error events.

```
videoView.setOnCompletionListener {
    // Called when the video playback completes
}
```

```
videoView.setOnErrorListener { _, _, _ ->
    // Called when an error occurs during video playback
    true // Return true to indicate that the error has been handled
}
```

Multimedia Best Practices

When working with multimedia elements in Android, consider the following best practices:

- Optimize multimedia files for size and quality to ensure efficient app performance.
- Provide playback controls and user feedback, such as play, pause, and volume controls.
- Use background services for long-running audio playback to allow the user to continue using the app.
- Handle exceptions and errors gracefully to prevent crashes or unexpected behavior when working with multimedia.

By effectively integrating audio and video elements into your Android app, you can create compelling multimedia experiences that engage and entertain your users.

6.5 Building a Simple Android Game

Creating games for Android can be an exciting and challenging endeavor. In this section, we'll explore how to build a simple Android game. While this won't cover complex game development topics, it will provide you with a basic understanding of game development on the Android platform.

Game Development Frameworks

Android game development often involves the use of game development frameworks and engines, such as Unity, Unreal Engine, or LibGDX. These frameworks provide a wide range of tools and features to simplify game development.

Unity

Unity is a popular cross-platform game engine that supports Android development. It provides a powerful editor, a vast asset store, and supports scripting in C#. Unity is known for its versatility and is suitable for both 2D and 3D game development.

LibGDX

LibGDX is a Java-based game development framework specifically designed for Android (as well as other platforms). It is lightweight, open-source, and offers a wide range of features for 2D game development.

Simple Android Game Example

Here, we'll provide a very basic example of building a simple Android game using Java and Android Studio. This example creates a "Tapping Game" where the player needs to tap a button as quickly as possible within a time limit.

1. **Create a New Android Project**: Start by creating a new Android project in Android Studio.

2. **Design the Game Layout**: Design the game layout in XML, which includes a button to tap and a countdown timer.

```
<Button
    android:id="@+id/tapButton"
    android:layout_width="wrap_content"
    android:layout_height="wrap_content"
    android:text="Tap Me!"
    android:layout_gravity="center"
    android:onClick="onTapButtonClicked" />

<TextView
    android:id="@+id/timerTextView"
    android:layout_width="wrap_content"
```

```
    android:layout_height="wrap_content"
    android:text="Time Left: 30"
    android:layout_gravity="center"
    android:layout_marginTop="16dp" />
```

3. **Implement the Game Logic**: In your Java code, implement the game logic. Start a countdown timer when the game starts, and update the score when the button is tapped.

```java
public class MainActivity extends AppCompatActivity {

    private Button tapButton;
    private TextView timerTextView;
    private int score = 0;
    private int timeLeft = 30; // Initial time limit in seconds

    @Override
    protected void onCreate(Bundle savedInstanceState) {
        super.onCreate(savedInstanceState);
        setContentView(R.layout.activity_main);

        tapButton = findViewById(R.id.tapButton);
        timerTextView = findViewById(R.id.timerTextView);

        // Start the game when the button is clicked
        tapButton.setOnClickListener(view -> startGame());
    }

    public void onTapButtonClicked(View view) {
        // Increment the score when the button is tapped
        score++;
        tapButton.setText("Score: " + score);
    }

    private void startGame() {
        // Reset the score and time
        score = 0;
        timeLeft = 30;
        tapButton.setText("Tap Me!");
        tapButton.setEnabled(true);

        // Start a countdown timer
        new CountDownTimer(30000, 1000) { // 30 seconds
            public void onTick(long millisUntilFinished) {
                timerTextView.setText("Time Left: " + timeLeft);
                timeLeft--;
            }

            public void onFinish() {
                timerTextView.setText("Game Over");
```

```
                    tapButton.setEnabled(false);
            }
        }.start();
    }
}
```

In this example, we define a simple tapping game where the player tries to tap the button as many times as possible within a 30-second time limit. When the game starts, a countdown timer begins, and the score increases each time the button is tapped. When the timer runs out, the game ends.

This is a basic illustration of how to create a simple Android game. For more complex games, you would typically use a game development framework or engine like Unity or LibGDX, which provide features for graphics rendering, physics, and more.

Remember that game development can become significantly more complex as you add features like graphics, sound, and complex gameplay mechanics. However, this example should give you a starting point for building your own Android games.

Chapter 7: Data Persistence in Android with Kotlin

Data persistence is a crucial aspect of Android app development. It involves storing and managing data so that it can be accessed and retrieved across different app sessions. In this chapter, we'll explore various data persistence techniques in Android using Kotlin.

7.1 SQLite Database in Android

SQLite is a lightweight, embedded relational database that comes bundled with Android. It provides a structured and efficient way to store and manage structured data within your Android apps. SQLite databases are commonly used for tasks like caching, storing user preferences, and maintaining app state.

Creating a SQLite Database

To work with SQLite databases in Android, you typically create a subclass of the SQLiteOpenHelper class. This subclass helps you manage database creation, version management, and provides access to the database.

Here's a basic example of how to create a SQLite database and define a table using Kotlin:

```kotlin
import android.content.Context
import android.database.sqlite.SQLiteDatabase
import android.database.sqlite.SQLiteOpenHelper

class MyDatabaseHelper(context: Context) : SQLiteOpenHelper(context, DATABASE
_NAME, null, DATABASE_VERSION) {

    companion object {
        private const val DATABASE_NAME = "myapp.db"
        private const val DATABASE_VERSION = 1
    }

    override fun onCreate(db: SQLiteDatabase) {
        // Create the table
        val createTableQuery = """
            CREATE TABLE IF NOT EXISTS my_table (
                _id INTEGER PRIMARY KEY AUTOINCREMENT,
                name TEXT,
                age INTEGER
            )
        """.trimIndent()

        db.execSQL(createTableQuery)
    }

    override fun onUpgrade(db: SQLiteDatabase, oldVersion: Int, newVersion: I
```

```
nt) {
        // Handle database upgrades if needed
    }
}
```

In this code, we create a `MyDatabaseHelper` class that extends `SQLiteOpenHelper`. The `onCreate` method is called when the database is created for the first time, and it defines the database schema by executing SQL statements.

Inserting and Retrieving Data

Once the database and table are defined, you can insert and retrieve data. Here's how you can insert data into the SQLite database:

```
val dbHelper = MyDatabaseHelper(context)
val db = dbHelper.writableDatabase

val values = ContentValues().apply {
    put("name", "John")
    put("age", 30)
}

val newRowId = db.insert("my_table", null, values)
```

To retrieve data from the database, you can use a query:

```
val projection = arrayOf("_id", "name", "age")
val sortOrder = "name DESC"

val cursor = db.query(
    "my_table", // The table to query
    projection, // The columns to return
    null,       // The columns for the WHERE clause (null means all rows)
    null,       // The values for the WHERE clause
    null,       // don't group the rows
    null,       // don't filter by row groups
    sortOrder   // The sort order
)

while (cursor.moveToNext()) {
    val itemId = cursor.getLong(cursor.getColumnIndexOrThrow("_id"))
    val name = cursor.getString(cursor.getColumnIndexOrThrow("name"))
    val age = cursor.getInt(cursor.getColumnIndexOrThrow("age"))
    // Do something with the data
}

cursor.close()
```

This code demonstrates how to query the database and retrieve data using a `Cursor`. You can then process the retrieved data as needed.

SQLite is a powerful tool for data persistence in Android, and it can handle a wide range of data storage needs. However, for more complex data structures or larger datasets, you may want to consider other persistence options like Room Database or SharedPreferences, which we'll explore in later sections.

7.2 Room Database Library

The Room Database Library is a modern and robust way to work with SQLite databases in Android. It provides a higher-level, more abstract interface for database operations and is part of the Android Jetpack library set. Room simplifies database management, reduces boilerplate code, and offers compile-time checks for SQL queries.

Setting up Room

To use Room in your Android project, you need to add the necessary dependencies to your app's build.gradle file:

```
implementation "androidx.room:room-runtime:2.4.0"
annotationProcessor "androidx.room:room-compiler:2.4.0"
```

Additionally, you should enable the AndroidX Jetifier and DataBinding in your project's gradle.properties file:

```
android.useAndroidX=true
android.enableJetifier=true
android.databinding.enableV2=true
```

Defining an Entity

In Room, you start by defining an entity class. An entity represents a table in your SQLite database. Each field in the entity class corresponds to a column in the table. Here's an example of defining an entity for a simple "User" table:

```
@Entity(tableName = "user")
data class User(
    @PrimaryKey(autoGenerate = true) val id: Long = 0,
    val name: String,
    val age: Int
)
```

In this example, the User class is annotated with @Entity, specifying the table name as "user." The @PrimaryKey annotation indicates that the "id" field is the primary key, and autoGenerate = true means that the primary key values will be automatically generated.

Creating a Database

Next, you create a Room database class that extends `RoomDatabase`. This class serves as the central access point to your app's data. You also define the entities and their corresponding DAOs (Data Access Objects) in this class. Here's an example:

```
@Database(entities = [User::class], version = 1)
abstract class AppDatabase : RoomDatabase() {
    abstract fun userDao(): UserDao
}
```

In this example, we define an `AppDatabase` class that includes a single entity, "User," and its corresponding DAO, `UserDao`.

Creating a DAO

The DAO is responsible for defining the methods that access the database. You create an interface annotated with `@Dao` and define methods for database operations. Here's an example of a `UserDao`:

```
@Dao
interface UserDao {
    @Query("SELECT * FROM user")
    fun getAllUsers(): List<User>

    @Insert
    fun insertUser(user: User)

    @Delete
    fun deleteUser(user: User)
}
```

In this example, the `UserDao` defines methods for querying all users, inserting a new user, and deleting a user.

Initializing and Using the Database

To use the Room database, you need to initialize it. Typically, you do this in your application's onCreate method:

```
val db = Room.databaseBuilder(
    applicationContext,
    AppDatabase::class.java, "app-database"
).build()
```

Once the database is initialized, you can use the DAOs to perform database operations:

```
val userDao = db.userDao()

val newUser = User(name = "Alice", age = 28)
userDao.insertUser(newUser)
```

```
val users = userDao.getAllUsers()
```

Room simplifies database operations by providing type-safe queries and compile-time checks. It also supports complex queries, relationships between entities, and LiveData for observing changes in the database.

Room is a powerful and recommended tool for data persistence in Android. It abstracts away many of the complexities of working directly with SQLite, making database management more efficient and less error-prone.

7.3 Shared Preferences

Shared Preferences is a simple and lightweight way to store small amounts of data as key-value pairs in Android. It is primarily used for storing app settings, user preferences, and other small pieces of data that need to persist across app sessions.

Using Shared Preferences

To work with Shared Preferences in Android, you first obtain a reference to the SharedPreferences object associated with your app's package name. Here's how you can get a SharedPreferences instance:

```
val sharedPref = context.getSharedPreferences(
    getString(R.string.preference_file_key), Context.MODE_PRIVATE
)
```

In this code, R.string.preference_file_key is a string resource that represents the name of the preference file. The Context.MODE_PRIVATE mode indicates that the preferences are private to the app and can't be accessed by other apps.

Writing Data to Shared Preferences

You can write data to Shared Preferences using editor objects. Here's an example of storing a string value:

```
with(sharedPref.edit()) {
    putString(getString(R.string.saved_high_score_key), "100")
    apply()
}
```

In this code, we obtain an editor object using sharedPref.edit() and then use methods like putString to store key-value pairs. The apply() method saves the changes asynchronously.

Reading Data from Shared Preferences

Reading data from Shared Preferences is straightforward. You can use methods like getString, getInt, getBoolean, etc., to retrieve values based on keys. Here's an example of retrieving a stored string value:

```
val highScore = sharedPref.getString(getString(R.string.saved_high_score_key)
, "0")
```

In this code, getString retrieves the value associated with the specified key. If the key doesn't exist, it returns the default value provided as the second parameter ("0" in this case).

Deleting Data

To remove data from Shared Preferences, you can use the remove method with the key you want to delete:

```
sharedPref.edit().remove(getString(R.string.saved_high_score_key)).apply()
```

SharedPreferences vs. Other Data Storage Options

Shared Preferences are suitable for small, simple data storage needs such as app settings and user preferences. However, they have limitations:

1. Limited Data Types: Shared Preferences support a limited set of data types (e.g., string, int, boolean).
2. Size Limitation: The amount of data you can store in Shared Preferences is limited, and it's not suitable for large datasets.
3. Lack of Structure: Shared Preferences do not provide a structured way to organize data.

For more complex data storage needs or larger datasets, consider other options like SQLite databases (covered in Section 7.1 and 7.2), which offer more flexibility and robustness.

In summary, Shared Preferences are a straightforward and efficient way to store small amounts of data in Android. They are commonly used for app settings and user preferences, making them a valuable tool for many Android applications.

7.4 Working with Files and Storage

Android provides several mechanisms for working with files and storage, allowing apps to save, read, and manage files. This section covers some common file and storage-related tasks in Android app development.

Internal Storage

Android apps have access to a private internal storage directory, which is not accessible to other apps or the user. You can use this storage for saving sensitive data or app-specific files.

To write a file to internal storage, you can use the following code:

```
val filename = "myfile.txt"
val fileContents = "Hello, this is my file content!"
val outputStream: FileOutputStream

try {
    outputStream = openFileOutput(filename, Context.MODE_PRIVATE)
    outputStream.write(fileContents.toByteArray())
    outputStream.close()
} catch (e: Exception) {
    e.printStackTrace()
}
```

In this example, we create a file named "myfile.txt" and write the content to it. The Context.MODE_PRIVATE flag ensures that the file is private to the app.

To read the content from this file, you can use the following code:

```
val filename = "myfile.txt"
val fileContents = try {
    openFileInput(filename).bufferedReader().use { it.readText() }
} catch (e: Exception) {
    e.printStackTrace()
    ""
}
```

External Storage

External storage in Android is a shared storage space that is readable and writable by multiple apps and accessible to the user. To use external storage, you need appropriate permissions and should check if it's available before using it.

Here's how you can check if external storage is writable:

```
val isExternalStorageWritable = Environment.getExternalStorageState() == Environment.MEDIA_MOUNTED
```

And here's how you can check if it's readable:

```
val isExternalStorageReadable = Environment.getExternalStorageState() in
        setOf(Environment.MEDIA_MOUNTED, Environment.MEDIA_MOUNTED_READ_ONLY)
```

To write to external storage, you can use code similar to what you'd use for internal storage, but you'll need to request the appropriate permissions, such as

WRITE_EXTERNAL_STORAGE. Be aware that starting with Android 10 (API level 29), you'll need to use scoped storage for accessing external storage.

Caching

Caching is a technique used to temporarily store data in a way that allows for quicker retrieval when needed. Android provides a built-in caching mechanism through the Cache directory. You can store files in the cache directory using the following code:

```
val cacheDir = context.cacheDir
val myFile = File(cacheDir, "myCacheFile.txt")

try {
    myFile.writeText("Cache this data for quick access!")
} catch (e: Exception) {
    e.printStackTrace()
}
```

Caching is particularly useful for storing temporary data that can be recreated if needed. The Android system may clear the cache when storage space is needed, so it's not suitable for critical or permanent data storage.

Conclusion

Working with files and storage is a fundamental part of Android app development. Whether you're saving user preferences, storing app-specific data, or managing files, understanding how to work with internal and external storage is essential for building robust Android applications. Additionally, consider using caching for temporary data to improve app performance.

7.5 Content Providers and Data Sharing

Content Providers are a fundamental component in Android that allow apps to share data with other apps securely. They act as an abstraction layer over data sources, such as databases, files, or network resources, and enable controlled access to this data. In this section, we'll explore how to use Content Providers for data sharing.

The Role of Content Providers

Content Providers offer a structured way to access and share data between apps. They encapsulate data access and retrieval methods, ensuring data integrity and security. Content Providers enable apps to expose data to other apps while enforcing data permissions and access rules.

Some common use cases for Content Providers include sharing contact information, accessing media files, sharing app-specific data, and exposing data from external sources like cloud storage.

Android provides several built-in Content Providers that allow access to system-level data. For example:

- The Contacts Provider (`ContactsContract`) allows apps to access and manipulate contact information.
- The Media Store Provider (`MediaStore`) provides access to media files, such as photos and videos.
- The Calendar Provider (`CalendarContract`) enables access to calendar events and scheduling.

To query data from a built-in Content Provider, you typically use a `ContentResolver`. Here's an example of querying contact information:

```
val contentResolver = context.contentResolver
val cursor = contentResolver.query(
    ContactsContract.Contacts.CONTENT_URI,
    null, null, null, null
)

if (cursor != null) {
    while (cursor.moveToNext()) {
        val name = cursor.getString(
            cursor.getColumnIndex(ContactsContract.Contacts.DISPLAY_NAME)
        )
        // Process contact data here
    }
    cursor.close()
}
```

Creating Custom Content Providers

In addition to using built-in Content Providers, you can create custom Content Providers for your app to share data with other apps. Creating a custom Content Provider involves defining a content URI, implementing data access methods, and defining the data schema.

Here's a high-level overview of creating a custom Content Provider:

1. Define a unique authority for your Content Provider, typically using your app's package name.
2. Define content URIs that specify the data you want to expose.
3. Implement data access methods like `query`, `insert`, `update`, and `delete`.
4. Define a data schema using a contract class to define table and column names.

Here's a simplified example of creating a custom Content Provider:

```
class MyContentProvider : ContentProvider() {

    override fun onCreate(): Boolean {
```

```kotlin
        // Initialize your Content Provider here
        return true
    }

    override fun query(
        uri: Uri, projection: Array<String>?, selection: String?,
        selectionArgs: Array<String>?, sortOrder: String?
    ): Cursor? {
        // Implement data retrieval here
        return null
    }

    override fun getType(uri: Uri): String? {
        // Define the MIME type for the data
        return null
    }

    override fun insert(uri: Uri, values: ContentValues?): Uri? {
        // Implement data insertion here
        return null
    }

    override fun update(uri: Uri, values: ContentValues?, selection: String?,
    selectionArgs: Array<String>?): Int {
        // Implement data update here
        return 0
    }

    override fun delete(uri: Uri, selection: String?, selectionArgs: Array<String>?): Int {
        // Implement data deletion here
        return 0
    }
}
```

Permissions and Data Access

Content Providers enforce data access permissions. To access data from a Content Provider, apps must have the appropriate permissions defined in their manifest files. Additionally, Content Providers can enforce read and write permissions for each data URI.

Conclusion

Content Providers are a crucial part of Android's data-sharing mechanism. Whether you're using built-in Content Providers or creating custom ones for your app, understanding how they work and how to define data access permissions is essential for building secure and collaborative Android applications.

Chapter 8: Networking and Web Services

8.1 Making HTTP Requests with Kotlin

In modern Android app development, making HTTP requests is a common task for fetching data from web services, APIs, or remote servers. Kotlin provides various libraries and methods to simplify the process of making HTTP requests. In this section, we will explore how to make HTTP requests in Kotlin and handle the responses.

Using the HTTP Client Libraries

Kotlin does not include a built-in HTTP client library, but you can use third-party libraries to make HTTP requests. One of the most commonly used libraries for this purpose is **OkHttp**, developed by Square. To use OkHttp in your Android project, you need to add it as a dependency in your app's build.gradle file:

```
implementation 'com.squareup.okhttp3:okhttp:4.9.1'
```

After adding the dependency, you can create an instance of OkHttp's OkHttpClient and use it to make HTTP requests. Here's an example of making a GET request to a URL and handling the response:

```kotlin
val client = OkHttpClient()

val request = Request.Builder()
    .url("https://api.example.com/data")
    .build()

client.newCall(request).enqueue(object : Callback {
    override fun onResponse(call: Call, response: Response) {
        val responseBody = response.body?.string()
        // Process the response data here
    }

    override fun onFailure(call: Call, e: IOException) {
        e.printStackTrace()
        // Handle the error here
    }
})
```

In this code, we create an OkHttpClient, build a GET request, and then enqueue the request asynchronously. When the response is received, the onResponse callback is called, allowing you to handle the response data. If an error occurs, the onFailure callback is invoked.

Handling JSON Responses

When dealing with web services and APIs, it's common to receive data in JSON format. To work with JSON data in Kotlin, you can use libraries like **Gson** to parse JSON responses into Kotlin objects. To use Gson, add it as a dependency in your app's build.gradle file:

```
implementation 'com.google.code.gson:gson:2.8.8'
```

Here's an example of parsing a JSON response into a Kotlin data class using Gson:

```
data class Post(val id: Int, val title: String, val body: String)

val gson = Gson()

val postJson = "{ \"id\": 1, \"title\": \"Sample Post\", \"body\": \"This is
a sample post.\" }"
val post = gson.fromJson(postJson, Post::class.java)

println("Post ID: ${post.id}")
println("Post Title: ${post.title}")
println("Post Body: ${post.body}")
```

In this code, we define a Post data class to match the JSON structure, and then we use Gson to parse the JSON string into a Post object.

Network Security

When making HTTP requests, it's essential to consider network security, especially when dealing with sensitive data. Android provides mechanisms for handling network security, such as using HTTPS for secure connections and implementing certificate pinning for added security.

Conclusion

Making HTTP requests in Android with Kotlin is a fundamental skill for building apps that interact with web services and APIs. Libraries like OkHttp and Gson simplify the process of sending and receiving data over the network, while also providing the flexibility to handle various types of requests and responses. Understanding network security best practices is crucial for ensuring the safety of your app's data communication.

8.2 JSON Parsing and Data Serialization

Working with JSON data is a common task when dealing with web services and APIs in Android development. JSON (JavaScript Object Notation) is a lightweight data interchange format that is easy to read and write. In this section, we'll explore how to parse JSON data in Kotlin and perform data serialization and deserialization.

Parsing JSON Data

To parse JSON data in Kotlin, you can use libraries like **Gson** or Android's built-in `JSONObject` and `JSONArray` classes. Gson is a popular choice due to its simplicity and flexibility.

Here's an example of parsing JSON data using Gson:

```kotlin
import com.google.gson.Gson

data class User(val id: Int, val name: String, val email: String)

val gson = Gson()

val json = "{\"id\": 1, \"name\": \"John\", \"email\": \"john@example.com\"}"

val user = gson.fromJson(json, User::class.java)

println("User ID: ${user.id}")
println("User Name: ${user.name}")
println("User Email: ${user.email}")
```

In this code, we define a `User` data class that matches the structure of the JSON data. We then use Gson's `fromJson` method to parse the JSON string into a `User` object.

Handling JSON Arrays

When dealing with JSON arrays, you can use `List` or `Array` types in Kotlin to store the parsed data. Here's an example of parsing a JSON array:

```kotlin
val jsonArray = "[{\"id\": 1, \"name\": \"John\"}, {\"id\": 2, \"name\": \"Alice\"}]"

val users = gson.fromJson(jsonArray, Array<User>::class.java)

for (user in users) {
    println("User ID: ${user.id}")
    println("User Name: ${user.name}")
}
```

In this code, we parse a JSON array containing user objects into an array of `User` objects.

Data Serialization

Data serialization is the process of converting objects into a format that can be easily transmitted or stored. Gson can also be used for data serialization, allowing you to convert Kotlin objects into JSON format.

Here's an example of serializing a Kotlin object into JSON:

```
val user = User(1, "Alice", "alice@example.com")

val json = gson.toJson(user)

println("Serialized User JSON: $json")
```

In this code, we use Gson's toJson method to serialize a User object into JSON format.

Custom Serialization and Deserialization

Gson provides customization options for handling complex JSON structures or non-standard JSON field names. You can create custom serializers and deserializers by implementing the JsonSerializer and JsonDeserializer interfaces.

Conclusion

Parsing JSON data and performing data serialization and deserialization are essential skills for Android developers when working with web services and APIs. Libraries like Gson simplify these tasks and provide flexibility in handling various JSON structures. Understanding how to work with JSON data ensures that your Android apps can communicate effectively with remote servers and services.

8.3 RESTful APIs and Retrofit Library

REST (Representational State Transfer) is a common architectural style for designing networked applications, and many web services and APIs follow RESTful principles. In this section, we'll explore RESTful APIs and how to work with them in Android using the Retrofit library.

Understanding RESTful APIs

RESTful APIs use standard HTTP methods (GET, POST, PUT, DELETE) to perform CRUD (Create, Read, Update, Delete) operations on resources identified by URLs. Resources are represented in a structured format, often using JSON or XML.

For example, consider a RESTful API for managing books:

- To retrieve a list of books, you might send a GET request to https://api.example.com/books.
- To create a new book, you might send a POST request with book data to the same URL.
- To update a specific book, you might send a PUT request to https://api.example.com/books/{id}.
- To delete a book, you might send a DELETE request to the book's URL.

Using Retrofit Library

Retrofit is a popular and powerful library for making HTTP requests and working with RESTful APIs in Android. It simplifies the process of defining API endpoints, sending requests, and handling responses.

To use Retrofit in your Android project, add it as a dependency in your app's build.gradle file:

```
implementation 'com.squareup.retrofit2:retrofit:2.9.0'
implementation 'com.squareup.retrofit2:converter-gson:2.9.0' // For Gson seri
alization
```

Here's a basic example of how to set up Retrofit and define an API interface:

```
import retrofit2.Call
import retrofit2.http.GET
import retrofit2.http.Path

data class Book(val id: Int, val title: String, val author: String)

interface BookApi {
    @GET("books")
    fun getBooks(): Call<List<Book>>

    @GET("books/{id}")
    fun getBookById(@Path("id") id: Int): Call<Book>
}
```

In this code, we define a `BookApi` interface with two methods: `getBooks` and `getBookById`. The `@GET` annotation specifies the HTTP method and relative URL for each endpoint.

To use the API, create a Retrofit instance and create a service using the interface:

```
val retrofit = Retrofit.Builder()
    .baseUrl("https://api.example.com/")
    .addConverterFactory(GsonConverterFactory.create())
    .build()

val bookApi = retrofit.create(BookApi::class.java)
```

Now you can use bookApi to make API requests and receive responses:

```
val call = bookApi.getBooks()
val response = call.execute()

if (response.isSuccessful) {
    val books = response.body()
    // Process the list of books
} else {
```

```
    // Handle error
}
```

Authentication and Headers

Retrofit supports various authentication mechanisms, including OAuth, API keys, and basic authentication. You can also add custom headers to your requests by defining them in the API interface methods.

Conclusion

Retrofit simplifies working with RESTful APIs in Android by providing a clean and efficient way to define API endpoints, send requests, and handle responses. Understanding how to use Retrofit is essential for building Android apps that interact with web services and APIs.

8.4 WebSocket Communication

WebSocket is a communication protocol that provides full-duplex, bidirectional communication channels over a single TCP connection. Unlike HTTP, which follows a request-response model, WebSocket allows both the client and server to send messages independently at any time. This makes WebSocket suitable for real-time applications such as chat applications, online gaming, and live notifications. In this section, we'll explore WebSocket communication in Android.

Understanding WebSocket

WebSocket communication starts with a handshake process, where the client and server establish a connection. Once the connection is established, both parties can send and receive messages without the overhead of opening and closing multiple HTTP connections.

WebSocket uses the ws or wss (WebSocket Secure) URI scheme for unencrypted and encrypted connections, respectively. The WebSocket protocol operates over the standard HTTP and HTTPS ports (80 and 443).

Using WebSocket in Android

To implement WebSocket communication in Android, you can use libraries such as **OkHttp** or **Java-WebSocket**. In this example, we'll use OkHttp, which is a widely adopted HTTP client library that also supports WebSocket.

First, add OkHttp as a dependency in your app's build.gradle file:

```
implementation 'com.squareup.okhttp3:okhttp:4.9.1'
```

Here's a basic example of how to create a WebSocket client using OkHttp:

```
import okhttp3.*
import java.util.concurrent.TimeUnit
```

```kotlin
class WebSocketClient {

    private val client = OkHttpClient.Builder()
        .readTimeout(0, TimeUnit.MILLISECONDS) // No timeout for read operati
ons
        .build()

    fun connect(url: String, listener: WebSocketListener) {
        val request = Request.Builder()
            .url(url)
            .build()

        client.newWebSocket(request, listener)
    }

    fun disconnect() {
        client.dispatcher().executorService().shutdown()
    }
}
```

In this code, we create a `WebSocketClient` class that uses OkHttp to manage WebSocket connections. The `connect` method establishes a WebSocket connection to the specified URL, and the `disconnect` method can be used to close the connection when no longer needed.

Creating a WebSocketListener

To handle WebSocket events, you need to create a `WebSocketListener`. This listener defines methods to handle events like connection success, message receipt, and disconnection. Here's an example of a simple `WebSocketListener`:

```kotlin
import okhttp3.Response
import okhttp3.WebSocket
import okhttp3.WebSocketListener
import okio.ByteString

class MyWebSocketListener : WebSocketListener() {
    override fun onOpen(webSocket: WebSocket, response: Response) {
        super.onOpen(webSocket, response)
        // Connection opened
    }

    override fun onMessage(webSocket: WebSocket, text: String) {
        super.onMessage(webSocket, text)
        // Text message received
    }

    override fun onMessage(webSocket: WebSocket, bytes: ByteString) {
        super.onMessage(webSocket, bytes)
```

```
        // Binary message received
    }

    override fun onClosing(webSocket: WebSocket, code: Int, reason: String) {
        super.onClosing(webSocket, code, reason)
        // Connection is closing
    }

    override fun onFailure(webSocket: WebSocket, t: Throwable, response: Response?) {
        super.onFailure(webSocket, t, response)
        // Connection failed
    }
}
```

In this code, we define the MyWebSocketListener class, which extends WebSocketListener and overrides the relevant methods to handle WebSocket events.

Connecting to a WebSocket Server

To use the WebSocket client, create an instance of WebSocketClient and call the connect method with the WebSocket server's URL and an instance of your WebSocketListener. For example:

```
val webSocketClient = WebSocketClient()
val serverUrl = "wss://example.com/chat"
val myListener = MyWebSocketListener()

webSocketClient.connect(serverUrl, myListener)
```

Now, your Android app is connected to the WebSocket server, and you can send and receive messages in real-time.

Sending and Receiving Messages

To send a message to the WebSocket server, use the send method on the WebSocket instance:

```
webSocket.send("Hello, server!")
```

To receive messages, handle the onMessage method in your WebSocketListener. Depending on the message format, you can process text or binary messages accordingly.

Disconnecting from the WebSocket Server

To gracefully close the WebSocket connection, call the disconnect method on the WebSocketClient:

```
webSocketClient.disconnect()
```

Conclusion

WebSocket communication is a powerful way to implement real-time features in Android applications. Libraries like OkHttp make it relatively straightforward to establish WebSocket connections and handle WebSocket events. Understanding how to use WebSocket in Android opens up possibilities for building interactive and real-time apps.

8.5 Integrating Third-Party APIs

Integrating third-party APIs into your Android app is a common practice that allows you to extend your app's functionality by leveraging external services and data sources. In this section, we'll explore the process of integrating third-party APIs into your Android application.

What are Third-Party APIs?

Third-party APIs (Application Programming Interfaces) are sets of rules and protocols that allow your app to communicate with external services, platforms, or data sources. These APIs are typically provided by third-party organizations or companies and can offer various functionalities, such as accessing data, performing actions, or interacting with services like social media platforms, payment gateways, and more.

Benefits of Integrating Third-Party APIs

Integrating third-party APIs can provide several benefits to your Android app:

1. **Access to External Data**: You can tap into a wealth of data and services without having to build them from scratch. For example, you can integrate weather APIs to provide real-time weather information to users.

2. **Enhanced Functionality**: Third-party APIs allow you to add features to your app that would otherwise be time-consuming or complex to develop on your own. This can include features like geolocation, authentication, or even machine learning capabilities.

3. **Efficiency**: Leveraging existing APIs can save development time and effort, as you can rely on well-documented and maintained solutions.

4. **Monetization**: Some APIs offer monetization opportunities through affiliate programs, advertising, or premium access tiers, which can generate revenue for your app.

Steps to Integrate Third-Party APIs

Here are the general steps to integrate third-party APIs into your Android app:

1. **Select an API**: Choose a third-party API that aligns with your app's requirements and objectives. Make sure to review the API's documentation, terms of use, and pricing, if applicable.

2. **Sign Up**: Create an account or register your app with the API provider to obtain an API key or credentials. This key is often required for authentication when making API requests.

3. **Read Documentation**: Thoroughly read the API documentation to understand how to make requests, what data is available, and how to handle responses.

4. **Implement API Requests**: In your Android app, implement the logic to make HTTP requests to the API using libraries like Retrofit, OkHttp, or Volley. Ensure that you handle errors and exceptions gracefully.

5. **Authentication**: If the API requires authentication, use the provided API key or authentication method when making requests. Keep your credentials secure and avoid hardcoding them in your app.

6. **Parse Responses**: Parse the JSON or XML responses from the API to extract the data you need. You may need to create data models that match the API's response structure.

7. **Error Handling**: Implement error handling to gracefully manage cases where the API is unavailable, returns errors, or exceeds rate limits.

8. **Testing**: Thoroughly test your app's integration with the third-party API in various scenarios, including both success and error cases.

9. **Optimize and Monitor**: Continuously monitor your app's usage of the API and optimize your implementation for performance and reliability. Be aware of any usage limitations or quotas imposed by the API provider.

10. **Compliance**: Ensure that your app complies with the terms of use and policies of the API provider, especially regarding data privacy and usage restrictions.

Examples of Third-Party APIs

There is a wide range of third-party APIs available for Android app integration. Some popular categories include:

- **Social Media APIs**: APIs provided by platforms like Facebook, Twitter, and Instagram for features such as sharing content, authentication, and accessing user data.

- **Payment APIs**: Payment gateways like PayPal and Stripe offer APIs for processing payments and managing transactions within your app.

- **Mapping and Location APIs**: Services like Google Maps provide APIs for displaying maps, geolocation, and directions in your app.

- **Weather APIs**: APIs from providers like OpenWeatherMap offer real-time weather data for your app's location-based features.

- **Authentication APIs**: Implement secure user authentication using third-party services like Firebase Authentication or OAuth providers.

- **Machine Learning APIs**: Integrate machine learning models and AI capabilities into your app using APIs like TensorFlow or IBM Watson.

- **E-commerce APIs**: Services like Amazon Product Advertising API enable you to access product data and monetize your app through affiliate marketing.

Conclusion

Integrating third-party APIs can significantly enhance the functionality and capabilities of your Android app. Careful selection, implementation, and ongoing maintenance of third-party APIs are crucial to ensure a smooth and reliable user experience while adhering to the terms and policies of API providers. Whether you want to add social sharing, payment processing, location services, or other features, third-party APIs offer a wealth of possibilities for expanding your app's capabilities.

Chapter 9: Building Location-Based Apps

9.1 Location Services in Android

Location-based apps have become an integral part of the mobile experience. They provide users with services and information tailored to their current location, such as maps, directions, local business recommendations, and geotagged social media posts. In this section, we'll delve into location services in Android and explore how to leverage them to create compelling location-based applications.

Understanding Location Services

Location services in Android rely on a combination of technologies, including Global Navigation Satellite Systems (GNSS) like GPS, network-based location services, and sensors like Wi-Fi and Bluetooth to determine a device's geographical coordinates (latitude and longitude). These services offer high-precision location information, making it possible to build apps that require accurate location data.

Location Providers

Android provides two main location providers:

1. **GPS Provider**: This provider uses the device's built-in GPS receiver to determine the location. It provides the most accurate location data but can consume significant power and may not work well indoors or in areas with limited GPS satellite visibility.

2. **Network Provider**: The network provider relies on cell towers and Wi-Fi signals to estimate the device's location. It is less accurate than GPS but works well in urban environments and indoors. It's also less power-hungry.

Permissions and API Integration

To access a device's location, your app must request the appropriate permissions from the user. Starting with Android 6.0 (API level 23), you must request location permissions at runtime.

Here's an example of how to request location permissions in your AndroidManifest.xml file:

```
<uses-permission android:name="android.permission.ACCESS_FINE_LOCATION" />
```

To integrate location services into your app, you can use Android's Location API, which provides classes like LocationManager and LocationListener for managing location updates. Here's a simplified example of how to request location updates:

```
// Acquire a reference to the system Location Manager
LocationManager locationManager = (LocationManager) getSystemService(Context.
LOCATION_SERVICE);
```

```java
// Define a Location Listener
LocationListener locationListener = new LocationListener() {
    public void onLocationChanged(Location location) {
        // Handle Location updates here
        double latitude = location.getLatitude();
        double longitude = location.getLongitude();
    }

    public void onStatusChanged(String provider, int status, Bundle extras) {
    }

    public void onProviderEnabled(String provider) {}

    public void onProviderDisabled(String provider) {}
};

// Request Location updates
if (ContextCompat.checkSelfPermission(this, Manifest.permission.ACCESS_FINE_L
OCATION)
        == PackageManager.PERMISSION_GRANTED) {
    locationManager.requestLocationUpdates(LocationManager.GPS_PROVIDER, 0, 0
, locationListener);
}
```

Location Accuracy and Battery Consumption

Location services can be a significant drain on a device's battery. To optimize battery usage, consider the following strategies:

- Use the appropriate location provider (GPS for high accuracy, network for less accuracy but lower power consumption).

- Minimize the frequency of location updates unless your app requires real-time tracking.

- Combine location updates with other sensors, such as the accelerometer, to detect when the device is stationary and reduce location polling.

- Use geofencing to trigger location updates only when the user enters or exits specific geographic areas of interest.

Geocoding and Reverse Geocoding

In addition to obtaining a device's current location, Android allows you to convert between geographic coordinates and human-readable addresses using geocoding and reverse geocoding. The Geocoder class provides methods to perform these conversions.

Location services open up numerous app development possibilities, including:

- **Maps and Navigation Apps**: Create apps that offer maps, turn-by-turn directions, and traffic information.

- **Local Business Finders**: Develop apps that help users find nearby restaurants, hotels, gas stations, and other businesses.

- **Geotagged Social Media**: Add location-based filters and features to social media apps to tag posts with location data.

- **Fitness and Health Tracking**: Build apps that track users' running routes, cycling paths, and hiking trails.

- **Augmented Reality**: Create AR apps that overlay information on the real world based on the user's location.

- **Emergency Services**: Develop apps that provide users with emergency services and information specific to their location.

Conclusion

Location services are a powerful tool for creating engaging and context-aware Android applications. Whether you're building navigation apps, location-based games, or services that rely on geographic data, a solid understanding of Android's location capabilities is essential. In the next sections, we'll explore more advanced topics in location-based app development, including GPS and geocoding in greater detail.

9.2 GPS and Geocoding

Global Positioning System (GPS) is a widely used technology for precise location determination on mobile devices. In this section, we'll delve into GPS in the context of Android app development and explore how to leverage it to obtain accurate location information.

Understanding GPS

GPS is a satellite-based navigation system that provides real-time geographic location data. Android devices have built-in GPS receivers that can communicate with a network of satellites to determine their latitude, longitude, altitude, and more. GPS is known for its high accuracy, making it ideal for applications that require precise location data, such as navigation and outdoor sports tracking apps.

GPS Permissions and Best Practices

To access GPS data in your Android app, you must request the appropriate permissions from the user. You can request the `ACCESS_FINE_LOCATION` permission in your app's AndroidManifest.xml file.

```
<uses-permission android:name="android.permission.ACCESS_FINE_LOCATION" />
```

Here are some best practices when working with GPS:

1. **Check GPS Availability**: Before requesting GPS location updates, check if GPS is available and enabled on the device. You can use the `LocationManager` class to do this.

2. **Minimize GPS Usage**: GPS is power-hungry. Minimize its usage by requesting updates only when necessary, and stop updates when they are no longer needed.

3. **Use GPS in Conjunction with Other Sensors**: Combine GPS data with other sensors, such as the accelerometer and gyroscope, to improve location accuracy and reduce power consumption.

4. **Geofencing**: Implement geofencing to trigger location updates when a user enters or exits specific geographic areas.

Obtaining GPS Location Updates

To obtain GPS location updates in your Android app, you can use the `LocationManager` class in conjunction with a `LocationListener`. Here's a simplified example of how to request GPS location updates:

```java
// Acquire a reference to the system Location Manager
LocationManager locationManager = (LocationManager) getSystemService(Context.LOCATION_SERVICE);

// Define a Location Listener
LocationListener locationListener = new LocationListener() {
    public void onLocationChanged(Location location) {
        // Handle location updates here
        double latitude = location.getLatitude();
        double longitude = location.getLongitude();
        // ...
    }

    // Other callback methods here
};

// Request GPS location updates
if (ContextCompat.checkSelfPermission(this, Manifest.permission.ACCESS_FINE_LOCATION)
        == PackageManager.PERMISSION_GRANTED) {
```

```
        locationManager.requestLocationUpdates(LocationManager.GPS_PROVIDER, 0, 0
, locationListener);
}
```

In addition to obtaining GPS coordinates, you can use geocoding and reverse geocoding to convert between geographic coordinates and human-readable addresses. The `Geocoder` class in Android provides methods to perform these conversions. Geocoding translates a location (latitude and longitude) into an address, while reverse geocoding converts an address into geographic coordinates.

GPS technology opens up a world of possibilities for app development, including:

- **Navigation Apps**: Create apps that provide turn-by-turn directions, traffic information, and real-time maps.

- **Fitness Trackers**: Build apps that track users' running, cycling, and hiking routes, along with statistics like distance, speed, and elevation.

- **Outdoor Adventure Guides**: Develop apps that assist outdoor enthusiasts with trail maps, points of interest, and safety information.

- **Location-Based Games**: Create augmented reality (AR) games that use GPS to overlay game elements on the real world.

- **Location-Based Social Networking**: Add location-based features to social media apps, allowing users to tag posts with their current location.

- **Emergency Services**: Develop apps that provide users with emergency services and location-specific information during crises.

GPS and geocoding are essential tools for building location-aware Android apps. Whether you're creating navigation apps, fitness trackers, or innovative location-based games, a solid understanding of GPS technology and best practices is crucial. In the next section, we'll explore maps and location-based user interfaces in greater detail, expanding on the concepts discussed here.

9.3 Maps and Location-based UI

Maps and location-based user interfaces (UI) play a pivotal role in many Android applications. This section explores how to integrate maps, display user locations, and create interactive location-based experiences in your Android apps.

Google Maps Integration

Google Maps is one of the most popular mapping services, and it offers a robust API for Android app integration. To include Google Maps in your Android app, you need to obtain an API key from the Google Cloud Console. Here's an overview of the steps to integrate Google Maps:

1. **Get an API Key**: Create a project in the Google Cloud Console, enable the Maps SDK for Android, and generate an API key.

2. **Add Dependencies**: In your app's `build.gradle` file, add the Google Maps dependency.

```
implementation 'com.google.android.gms:play-services-maps:17.0.1'
```

3. **Configure the Manifest**: In your AndroidManifest.xml file, add the following metadata element with your API key:

```
<meta-data
    android:name="com.google.android.geo.API_KEY"
    android:value="YOUR_API_KEY" />
```

4. **Initialize Google Maps**: In your app code, initialize the Google Maps SDK by calling `MapsInitializer.initialize(context)`.

Now, you can display maps, markers, and other interactive features in your app.

Displaying User Location

To display the user's current location on a map, you can use the `GoogleMap` object and the `LocationServices` API. Here's a simplified example of how to do this:

```
// Get a reference to the GoogleMap object
GoogleMap map = googleMap;

// Enable the My Location layer, which shows the user's location on the map
if (ContextCompat.checkSelfPermission(this, Manifest.permission.ACCESS_FINE_L
OCATION)
        == PackageManager.PERMISSION_GRANTED) {
    map.setMyLocationEnabled(true);
} else {
    // Request location permission
    ActivityCompat.requestPermissions(this, new String[]{Manifest.permission.
ACCESS_FINE_LOCATION}, PERMISSION_REQUEST_CODE);
}

// Get the user's last known location
FusedLocationProviderClient fusedLocationClient = LocationServices.getFusedLo
cationProviderClient(this);
fusedLocationClient.getLastLocation()
    .addOnSuccessListener(this, location -> {
```

```
        if (location != null) {
            // Use the user's last known location
            double latitude = location.getLatitude();
            double longitude = location.getLongitude();
            LatLng userLocation = new LatLng(latitude, longitude);
            map.moveCamera(CameraUpdateFactory.newLatLngZoom(userLocation, 15
));
        }
    });
```

Adding Markers and Overlays

You can enhance your maps by adding markers, overlays, and custom elements. For example, to add a marker to a specific location, use the following code:

```
LatLng markerLocation = new LatLng(37.7749, -122.4194);
MarkerOptions markerOptions = new MarkerOptions()
        .position(markerLocation)
        .title("San Francisco");
map.addMarker(markerOptions);
```

Geofencing

Geofencing is a location-based feature that allows you to define virtual geographic boundaries and trigger actions when a device enters or exits these boundaries. It's useful for creating location-aware apps with context-aware behaviors. Android provides the GeofencingClient class for managing geofences.

Location-based UI

Location-based UI design involves adapting your app's user interface based on the user's location. For example, you can show different content or options to users depending on whether they are indoors or outdoors, in a specific city, or near a landmark.

Conclusion

Maps and location-based UI elements add valuable functionality and interactivity to Android apps. Whether you're building a travel app, a restaurant finder, or a fitness tracker, integrating maps and location services can significantly enhance the user experience. In the next section, we'll delve into location permissions and best practices to ensure that your app respects user privacy and operates smoothly.

9.4 Location Permissions and Best Practices

Location-based features are powerful tools in Android apps, but they come with a responsibility to respect user privacy and provide a seamless user experience. In this section, we'll discuss location permissions, best practices, and guidelines for building apps that use location services.

Requesting Location Permissions

Before accessing a user's location, your app must request permission. Starting with Android 6.0 (API level 23), apps must explicitly request location permissions at runtime. Here's how you can request location permission:

```
// Check if permission is already granted
if (ContextCompat.checkSelfPermission(this, Manifest.permission.ACCESS_FINE_LOCATION)
        != PackageManager.PERMISSION_GRANTED) {

    // Permission is not granted, request it
    ActivityCompat.requestPermissions(this,
            new String[]{Manifest.permission.ACCESS_FINE_LOCATION},
            LOCATION_PERMISSION_REQUEST_CODE);
} else {
    // Permission is already granted, proceed with location access
}
```

Ensure that you explain to users why your app needs their location and request permission only when necessary. Handle the user's response to the permission request using onRequestPermissionsResult.

Location Providers

Android devices can determine location through various providers, including GPS, network, and fused location. Use the most appropriate provider for your app's needs, considering factors like accuracy and power consumption. You can check if location services are enabled and available:

```
LocationManager locationManager = (LocationManager) getSystemService(Context.LOCATION_SERVICE);
if (!locationManager.isProviderEnabled(LocationManager.GPS_PROVIDER)
        && !locationManager.isProviderEnabled(LocationManager.NETWORK_PROVIDER)) {
    // Location services are not enabled, prompt the user to enable them
}
```

Battery Efficiency

Location updates can significantly impact battery life. To conserve power, follow these practices:

- **Minimize Location Requests**: Request location updates only when your app needs them. Use appropriate intervals and conditions to reduce the frequency of updates.

- **Opt for Fused Location Provider**: The Fused Location Provider combines data from various sources to provide accurate and power-efficient location updates. Consider using it over GPS or network providers.

- **Remove Updates When Not Needed**: When your app no longer requires location updates, remove the request to stop consuming resources.

```
// Remove location updates
LocationServices.getFusedLocationProviderClient(this).removeLocationUpdates(l
ocationCallback);
```

Handling Location Changes

Android devices can experience location changes due to various factors, such as moving between Wi-Fi networks, GPS signal fluctuations, or transitioning between indoor and outdoor environments. Your app should gracefully handle location changes to provide a consistent user experience.

Testing Location-Aware Features

When testing location-aware features, use tools like the Android Emulator to simulate different locations and movement. This allows you to test how your app behaves under various conditions without physically moving.

Privacy Considerations

Location data is sensitive. Always inform users how their location data will be used and provide options to control location settings within your app. Follow Google's privacy guidelines for location-based apps to ensure compliance with best practices.

Conclusion

Location-based features are valuable for many Android apps, but they must be implemented with care and consideration for user privacy and device resources. By following best practices for location permissions, provider selection, battery efficiency, and privacy, you can create location-aware apps that enhance the user experience without compromising privacy or draining device batteries.

9.5 Geofencing and Location Awareness

Geofencing is a powerful location-based technique that allows you to define virtual boundaries or regions in the real world. When a device enters or exits these predefined geofences, your app can receive notifications and perform specific actions. In this section, we will explore geofencing and how to implement it in your Android app.

What Is Geofencing?

Geofencing is a technology that uses GPS or other location data to trigger actions when a device enters or exits a specific geographic area. Geofences can be circular or polygonal and are defined by latitude and longitude coordinates. Common use cases for geofencing include location-based reminders, tracking user activity, and delivering location-specific content.

Implementing Geofencing in Android

To implement geofencing in your Android app, you'll need to use the Google Play Services Location APIs. Here's a high-level overview of the steps involved:

1. **Add Dependencies**: Include the necessary dependencies in your project's build.gradle file.

```
dependencies {
    implementation 'com.google.android.gms:play-services-location:18.0.0'
}
```

2. **Request Location Permissions**: As discussed in the previous sections, ensure that you have the required location permissions.

3. **Create Geofences**: Define the geofences you want to monitor by specifying their coordinates, radius, and other parameters.

```
Geofence geofence = new Geofence.Builder()
        .setRequestId("my-geofence-id")
        .setCircularRegion(latitude, longitude, radiusInMeters)
        .setExpirationDuration(Geofence.NEVER_EXPIRE)
        .setTransitionTypes(Geofence.GEOFENCE_ENTER | Geofence.GEOFENCE_EXIT)
        .build();
```

4. **Register Geofences**: Register the geofences with the GeofencingClient.

```
GeofencingClient geofencingClient = LocationServices.getGeofencingClient(this);
geofencingClient.addGeofences(getGeofencingRequest(geofence), getGeofencePend
ingIntent())
        .addOnSuccessListener(this, aVoid -> {
            // Geofences added successfully
        })
        .addOnFailureListener(this, e -> {
            // Geofences failed to be added
        });
```

5. **Handle Geofence Transitions**: Implement a PendingIntent to handle geofence transitions, such as entry or exit.

6. **Receive Geofence Events**: When the device enters or exits a geofence, your app will receive an Intent in the specified PendingIntent.

```
public class GeofenceBroadcastReceiver extends BroadcastReceiver {
    @Override
    public void onReceive(Context context, Intent intent) {
        GeofencingEvent geofencingEvent = GeofencingEvent.fromIntent(intent);
        if (geofencingEvent.hasError()) {
            // Handle the error
        } else {
            int transitionType = geofencingEvent.getGeofenceTransition();
```

```java
        if (transitionType == Geofence.GEOFENCE_TRANSITION_ENTER) {
            // Handle geofence entry
        } else if (transitionType == Geofence.GEOFENCE_TRANSITION_EXIT) {
            // Handle geofence exit
        }
    }
  }
}
```

7. **Remove Geofences**: When you no longer need to monitor a geofence, remove it to conserve resources.

Best Practices for Geofencing

- Use geofencing for relevant and valuable notifications to avoid annoying users.

- Be mindful of battery usage by optimizing geofence size and accuracy.

- Handle geofence transitions gracefully and provide a clear user experience.

- Test your geofencing implementation thoroughly to ensure it works as expected.

- Respect user privacy and only collect location data when necessary.

Conclusion

Geofencing is a versatile tool for adding location awareness to your Android app. By implementing geofences and handling geofence transitions effectively, you can create context-aware experiences and deliver location-specific content to users. However, it's crucial to use geofencing responsibly and consider battery optimization and user privacy when implementing this feature.

Chapter 10: Handling Background Tasks and Services

10.1 Android Services and Background Execution

In Android app development, you often encounter scenarios where you need to perform tasks in the background without blocking the user interface (UI). Android provides several mechanisms for handling background tasks, and one of the fundamental components for this purpose is **Services**.

What Are Android Services?

An Android **Service** is a component that runs in the background to perform long-running operations without a user interface. Services are often used for tasks such as downloading files, playing music, handling network requests, or performing periodic updates. There are two main types of services:

1. **Foreground Services**: These services are visible to the user and provide ongoing notifications in the notification bar, indicating that a background task is running. Foreground services are typically used for tasks that the user is aware of and wants to keep running, such as playing music or navigation.

2. **Background Services**: These services run in the background without a visible UI or user notifications. They are suitable for tasks that don't require direct user interaction but need to continue even if the app is in the background or not running.

Creating a Service

To create a service in Android, you need to create a subclass of the `Service` class and override its lifecycle methods. Here's a basic example:

```
public class MyService extends Service {

    @Override
    public void onCreate() {
        super.onCreate();
        // Initialization code when the service is created.
    }

    @Override
    public int onStartCommand(Intent intent, int flags, int startId) {
        // Code to start and run the background task.
        return START_STICKY; // Specifies how the service should behave after
being killed.
    }

    @Override
    public void onDestroy() {
```

```java
        super.onDestroy();
        // Cleanup code when the service is destroyed.
    }

    @Nullable
    @Override
    public IBinder onBind(Intent intent) {
        // Return null if the service is not meant to be bound.
        return null;
    }
}
```

Starting a Service

You can start a service using an Intent. Depending on your needs, you can start a service as a one-time operation or keep it running until you explicitly stop it. Here's how to start a service:

```java
Intent serviceIntent = new Intent(context, MyService.class);
context.startService(serviceIntent);
```

Stopping a Service

To stop a service, you can use the stopService() method or call stopSelf() from within the service itself. Here's how to stop a service:

```java
Intent serviceIntent = new Intent(context, MyService.class);
context.stopService(serviceIntent);
```

Foreground Services

To create a foreground service, you need to provide a notification that represents the ongoing operation. This notification keeps the service running in the foreground even when the app is not in the foreground. Foreground services are ideal for tasks that the user should be aware of, like music playback or navigation. Here's how to create a foreground service:

```java
public class MyForegroundService extends Service {

    @Override
    public void onCreate() {
        super.onCreate();
        // Initialization code for the foreground service.
        startForeground(NOTIFICATION_ID, createNotification());
    }

    // Other lifecycle methods and service logic.

    private Notification createNotification() {
        // Create and configure a notification for the foreground service.
```

```
        }
}
```

Background Service Best Practices

When working with background services, consider the following best practices:

- **Use background services for tasks that need to run independently of the app's lifecycle.**

- **Optimize resource usage**: Ensure that your background service doesn't consume excessive CPU, memory, or battery. Be mindful of device resources.

- **Handle errors and crashes gracefully**: Implement error handling and logging to detect and recover from errors in your background tasks.

- **Use WorkManager**: For background tasks that need to be deferred or scheduled, consider using the Android WorkManager API, which provides a more flexible and efficient way to manage background work.

- **Foreground services for user awareness**: If a background task requires user awareness or interaction, use a foreground service with a notification to keep the user informed.

Conclusion

Background services are a crucial part of Android development, enabling apps to perform tasks in the background while ensuring a smooth user experience. Whether you need to download files, sync data, or perform periodic updates, understanding how to create and manage Android services is essential for building robust Android applications. In the next sections, we'll explore other mechanisms for handling background tasks, such as AsyncTask, JobScheduler, and WorkManager.

10.2 AsyncTask and Thread Management

In Android app development, managing background tasks efficiently is essential for maintaining a responsive user interface and preventing application freezes. One of the traditional approaches for handling background tasks is through the use of AsyncTask. While AsyncTask can be straightforward for simple tasks, it has limitations and should be used with caution.

Introduction to AsyncTask

AsyncTask is a class provided by the Android framework that simplifies working with background threads and updating the UI thread. It allows you to perform background tasks and publish results on the UI thread without the need to manage threads manually. An AsyncTask consists of three main methods:

1. **doInBackground(Params...)**: This method is executed on a background thread and is where you perform the actual background work. You pass input parameters (if needed) and return results.

2. **onPostExecute(Result)**: This method is called on the UI thread after doInBackground completes. It receives the result from the background task and can be used to update the UI.

3. **onProgressUpdate(Progress...)**: If you need to update the UI with intermediate progress, you can call publishProgress from doInBackground, and this method will be invoked on the UI thread with the progress values.

Using AsyncTask

Here's a basic example of using AsyncTask to perform a simple background task:

```java
private class MyTask extends AsyncTask<Void, Void, String> {

    @Override
    protected String doInBackground(Void... voids) {
        // Background task: perform time-consuming operation here.
        return "Task completed";
    }

    @Override
    protected void onPostExecute(String result) {
        // UI thread: update UI with the result.
        textView.setText(result);
    }
}
```

You can execute this task as follows:

```java
MyTask myTask = new MyTask();
myTask.execute();
```

AsyncTask Limitations

While AsyncTask is convenient for simple background tasks, it has limitations that make it less suitable for more complex scenarios:

1. **Limited control over thread management**: AsyncTask internally manages a pool of background threads, which can lead to issues with thread starvation and thread pool exhaustion in certain cases.

2. **Lifecycle-related issues**: AsyncTask can be problematic when dealing with configuration changes (e.g., screen rotation) because it may reference the old Activity after a configuration change.

3. **Not suitable for long-running tasks**: AsyncTask is designed for short-lived tasks. It's not suitable for tasks that may take a long time to complete, such as downloading large files or continuous network requests.

Alternatives to AsyncTask

For more robust background task management, consider using alternatives like the Android ViewModel with LiveData or the Android Architecture Components. These provide better control over the lifecycle and are suitable for more complex scenarios.

Additionally, the Android Executor framework and Thread class offer more flexibility and control over thread management. Using these options allows you to tailor your background task handling to the specific requirements of your app.

In summary, while AsyncTask is a straightforward way to handle simple background tasks in Android, it has limitations that make it less suitable for more complex scenarios. It's essential to evaluate the requirements of your app and choose the most appropriate background task management approach to ensure a smooth user experience.

10.3 JobScheduler and WorkManager

Android provides two powerful APIs, JobScheduler and WorkManager, for managing background tasks and services more efficiently, especially in scenarios where you need precise control over task execution, scheduling, and optimization of system resources.

JobScheduler

JobScheduler is a system service introduced in Android 5.0 (API level 21) that allows you to schedule tasks or jobs to run under certain conditions. It is a flexible and intelligent way to schedule background tasks while taking into account factors like battery optimization and network connectivity.

Here's how you can use JobScheduler:

1. **Create a JobService**: You need to create a subclass of JobService to define the work to be done in the background. Override the onStartJob() method to perform the task and return true if there's more work to be done, or false if the job is complete.

```
public class MyJobService extends JobService {
    @Override
    public boolean onStartJob(JobParameters params) {
        // Background task: perform work here.
        return false; // Return false if the job is complete.
    }

    @Override
    public boolean onStopJob(JobParameters params) {
```

```
        // Called if the job is interrupted before completion.
        return true; // Reschedule the job.
    }
}
```

2. **Schedule the Job**: To schedule the job, you create a JobInfo object and use the JobScheduler service to schedule it. You specify conditions like network connectivity, charging status, and more.

```
ComponentName componentName = new ComponentName(context, MyJobService.c
lass);
JobInfo jobInfo = new JobInfo.Builder(JOB_ID, componentName)
    .setRequiresCharging(true)
    .setRequiredNetworkType(JobInfo.NETWORK_TYPE_UNMETERED)
    .setPeriodic(15 * 60 * 1000) // 15 minutes
    .build();

JobScheduler jobScheduler = (JobScheduler) context.getSystemService(Con
text.JOB_SCHEDULER_SERVICE);
jobScheduler.schedule(jobInfo);
```

WorkManager

WorkManager is a more modern and recommended approach for background task management, introduced in Android Architecture Components. It builds upon JobScheduler and provides additional benefits:

- **Backward compatibility**: WorkManager is compatible with devices running Android 4.0 (API level 14) and higher.

- **Guaranteed execution**: It ensures that tasks are executed even if the app is killed or the device is rebooted.

- **Chainable tasks**: You can define complex task chains and dependencies between them.

Here's how you can use WorkManager:

1. **Create a Worker**: You create a subclass of Worker to define the background work to be done.

```
public class MyWorker extends Worker {
    public MyWorker(
        @NonNull Context context,
        @NonNull WorkerParameters workerParams
    ) {
        super(context, workerParams);
    }

    @NonNull
```

```
    @Override
    public Result doWork() {
        // Background task: perform work here.
        return Result.success(); // Return Result.success() for success
or Result.failure() for failure.
    }
}
```

2. **Define a WorkRequest**: You create a WorkRequest to specify the work to be done and its constraints.

```
OneTimeWorkRequest workRequest = new OneTimeWorkRequest.Builder(MyWorke
r.class)
    .setConstraints(
        Constraints.Builder()
            .setRequiresCharging(true)
            .setRequiredNetworkType(NetworkType.UNMETERED)
            .build()
    )
    .build();
```

3. **Enqueue the WorkRequest**: You enqueue the WorkRequest to the WorkManager to schedule the task.

```
WorkManager.getInstance(context).enqueue(workRequest);
```

Choosing Between JobScheduler and WorkManager

When deciding between JobScheduler and WorkManager, consider the following:

- Use WorkManager for its backward compatibility and guaranteed execution, especially if you need to support older Android versions.

- If your app targets Android 5.0 (API level 21) and higher and you want precise control over job scheduling and conditions, JobScheduler is a suitable choice.

Both JobScheduler and WorkManager are powerful tools for managing background tasks efficiently in Android apps, and your choice should depend on your app's requirements and target audience.

10.4 Push Notifications

Push notifications are a crucial feature for engaging users and keeping them informed about updates, messages, and events in your Android app, even when the app is not actively running. In this section, we'll explore how to implement push notifications in your Android application.

Push notifications are messages that your server sends to your app, and the Android device displays them in the system tray. Users can tap on these notifications to open your app or perform specific actions. Push notifications are typically used for:

- **Messaging**: Informing users about new messages, chat updates, or social interactions.
- **Updates**: Notifying users about new content, app updates, or important announcements.
- **Events**: Reminding users of upcoming events, appointments, or deadlines.
- **Marketing**: Promoting products, offers, or special deals to engage users.

Implementing Push Notifications

To implement push notifications in your Android app, you can use Firebase Cloud Messaging (FCM) or other cloud-based notification services. Here's a general outline of the steps involved:

1. **Set Up Firebase**: If you're using FCM, create a Firebase project in the Firebase Console (https://console.firebase.google.com/). Add your Android app to the project and download the `google-services.json` file.

2. **Integrate FCM SDK**: Add the Firebase Cloud Messaging SDK to your Android project by including the `google-services.json` file in your app module and configuring your app-level `build.gradle` file.

   ```
   apply plugin: 'com.google.gms.google-services'
   ```

3. **Request Permissions**: In your app's manifest file, request the necessary permissions for handling notifications.

   ```
   <uses-permission android:name="android.permission.INTERNET" />
   <uses-permission android:name="android.permission.WAKE_LOCK" />
   <uses-permission android:name="com.google.android.c2dm.permission.RECEI
   VE" />
   ```

4. **Create a Notification Channel (Android 8.0+)**: For Android 8.0 (API level 26) and higher, you should create a notification channel to group and manage your notifications effectively.

   ```
   if (Build.VERSION.SDK_INT >= Build.VERSION_CODES.O) {
       NotificationChannel channel = new NotificationChannel(
           "channel_id",
           "Channel Name",
           NotificationManager.IMPORTANCE_DEFAULT
       );
       NotificationManager manager = getSystemService(NotificationManager.
   class);
   ```

```
        manager.createNotificationChannel(channel);
    }
```

5. **Register for Push Notifications**: In your app, register the device to receive push notifications from the FCM service. This typically involves calling the `FirebaseMessaging.getInstance().subscribeToTopic(topic)` method.

6. **Handle Incoming Notifications**: Implement a `FirebaseMessagingService` to handle incoming notifications. Override the `onMessageReceived` method to customize the behavior when a notification is received.

```
public class MyFirebaseMessagingService extends FirebaseMessagingServic
e {
    @Override
    public void onMessageReceived(RemoteMessage remoteMessage) {
        // Handle the incoming notification message.
    }
}
```

7. **Display Notifications**: When you receive a push notification, create and display a notification in the system tray. Use the `NotificationManager` to build and show notifications.

```
NotificationCompat.Builder builder = new NotificationCompat.Builder(thi
s, "channel_id")
    .setSmallIcon(R.drawable.notification_icon)
    .setContentTitle("Notification Title")
    .setContentText("Notification Text")
    .setPriority(NotificationCompat.PRIORITY_DEFAULT);

NotificationManagerCompat notificationManager = NotificationManagerComp
at.from(this);
notificationManager.notify(notificationId, builder.build());
```

8. **Customize Notifications**: You can customize notifications by adding actions, sound, vibration, and more to provide a rich user experience.

Conclusion

Push notifications are a powerful way to engage users and keep them informed about important events in your Android app. Implementing push notifications using services like Firebase Cloud Messaging can help you deliver timely and relevant messages to your users, enhancing their overall experience with your app.

10.5 Syncing Data in the Background

Synchronization of data in the background is a crucial aspect of many Android applications, especially those that rely on real-time data updates, offline access, or collaborative features.

In this section, we will explore various strategies and techniques for syncing data efficiently in the background.

Background data synchronization ensures that your app remains up-to-date with the latest information without requiring constant user interaction. It serves several purposes:

1. **Real-time Updates**: Users expect timely updates without having to manually refresh content.

2. **Offline Access**: Background sync enables offline access to previously fetched data, improving the user experience.

3. **Battery Efficiency**: Efficient background sync reduces battery consumption by batching and optimizing data transfers.

4. **Collaborative Features**: In collaborative apps, background sync allows users to work together seamlessly.

Strategies for Background Data Sync

1. WorkManager

WorkManager is a powerful Android library for managing background tasks, including data synchronization. It offers features like job queuing, scheduling, and the ability to run tasks even when the app is in the background.

```
// Define a OneTimeWorkRequest to sync data
OneTimeWorkRequest dataSyncWorkRequest = new OneTimeWorkRequest.Builder(DataS
yncWorker.class)
    .setInitialDelay(15, TimeUnit.MINUTES) // Delay before running the task
    .build();

// Enqueue the work request
WorkManager.getInstance(context).enqueue(dataSyncWorkRequest);
```

2. SyncAdapter

SyncAdapter is an Android component designed specifically for background data synchronization. It allows you to define the sync logic and schedule periodic syncs with the server.

```
// Create a SyncAdapter instance
SyncAdapter syncAdapter = new SyncAdapter(getApplicationContext(), true);

// Request a sync
syncAdapter.requestSync(account, authority, extras);
```

3. Firebase Cloud Firestore

If your app uses Firebase, Firestore provides real-time synchronization out of the box. It automatically syncs data between the server and devices when changes occur.

```
// Listen for changes in a Firestore document
DocumentReference docRef = db.collection("cities").document("SF");
docRef.addSnapshotListener((snapshot, e) -> {
    if (e != null) {
        Log.w(TAG, "Listen failed.", e);
        return;
    }

    if (snapshot != null && snapshot.exists()) {
        Log.d(TAG, "Current data: " + snapshot.getData());
    } else {
        Log.d(TAG, "Current data: null");
    }
});
```

Best Practices

When implementing background data sync in your Android app, consider the following best practices:

1. **Use Network Constraints**: Ensure that data sync tasks run only when the device has an active network connection to avoid unnecessary battery drain.

2. **Batch Updates**: Minimize the number of network requests by batching data updates whenever possible.

3. **Error Handling**: Implement robust error handling and retry mechanisms to handle sync failures gracefully.

4. **Battery Optimization**: Optimize data sync tasks to reduce battery consumption and minimize wake locks.

5. **UI Feedback**: Provide clear feedback to users when background sync is in progress or when errors occur.

6. **Testing**: Thoroughly test background sync functionality, including scenarios like poor network conditions and device reboots.

Background data synchronization is a fundamental aspect of many modern Android apps. Implementing it effectively ensures that your app provides a seamless and up-to-date experience for users, even when they are not actively using the app.

Chapter 11: Security and Permissions

Section 11.1: Android Permissions System

Android permissions are a fundamental aspect of Android app development. They determine the actions that an app can perform and the access it has to user data and device resources. Understanding the Android permissions system is crucial for building secure and privacy-respecting applications.

Introduction to Android Permissions

Android permissions are safeguards that help protect user privacy and device security. Each permission represents a specific access right, such as reading contacts, accessing the camera, or using the device's location. When an app requests a permission, the user is presented with a permission request dialog explaining why the permission is needed. The user can then choose to grant or deny the permission.

Permission Groups

Permissions are organized into groups to make the permission request process more user-friendly. For example, the CAMERA permission belongs to the "Camera" permission group, and the READ_CONTACTS permission is part of the "Contacts" permission group. Requesting permissions at the group level is more straightforward for users, as they can understand why an app needs access to a particular resource.

Declaring Permissions in the Manifest

To request permissions, you must declare them in your app's AndroidManifest.xml file. This declaration informs the Android system and the user about the permissions your app needs. For example:

```xml
<uses-permission android:name="android.permission.CAMERA" />
<uses-permission android:name="android.permission.READ_CONTACTS" />
```

Runtime Permission Requests

Starting with Android 6.0 (API level 23), apps must request certain permissions at runtime. This means that even if you declare a permission in the manifest, you must also check if the permission is granted at runtime before using it. If it's not granted, you must request it from the user.

Handling Permission Responses

When a user responds to a permission request, your app receives the result in the onRequestPermissionsResult method. You can then handle the user's choice, which can be either granting or denying the permission. It's essential to provide clear and informative explanations about why your app needs the requested permissions to gain the user's trust.

Here are some best practices for handling Android permissions:

1. **Explain Why**: Always explain why your app needs a particular permission. Users are more likely to grant permissions when they understand the purpose.

2. **Request Permissions When Needed**: Request permissions at the point in your app where they are required, not all at once when the app starts.

3. **Handle Denials Gracefully**: Handle cases where users deny permissions gracefully. Explain the consequences and limitations to the user.

4. **Check Permissions Before Use**: Before accessing a protected resource, check if the required permission is granted. If not, request it.

5. **Test with Different Permission Scenarios**: Test your app under various permission scenarios to ensure it behaves correctly when permissions are denied.

6. **Request Permissions Tactfully**: Avoid overwhelming users with permission requests. Request permissions gradually as the user navigates through your app.

Understanding and managing Android permissions is a crucial part of app development, and it's essential to strike a balance between providing a seamless user experience and ensuring user privacy and security.

Section 11.2: Handling User Permissions

In Android app development, handling user permissions effectively is crucial for providing a smooth user experience and ensuring that your app complies with privacy and security standards. This section covers various aspects of handling user permissions in Android apps.

Requesting Permissions at Runtime

Starting from Android 6.0 (API level 23), Android introduced the concept of runtime permissions. This means that even if you declare permissions in the AndroidManifest.xml file, you need to request them at runtime when the app is running. To request permissions, follow these steps:

1. Check if the permission is already granted:

```
if (ContextCompat.checkSelfPermission(this, Manifest.permission.CAMERA)
== PackageManager.PERMISSION_GRANTED) {
    // Permission is already granted, perform the required action.
} else {
    // Permission is not granted; request it.
    ActivityCompat.requestPermissions(this, arrayOf(Manifest.permission
```

```
    .CAMERA), CAMERA_PERMISSION_REQUEST_CODE)
    }
```

2.   Handle the permission request response:

```
override fun onRequestPermissionsResult(requestCode: Int, permissions:
Array<out String>, grantResults: IntArray) {
    when (requestCode) {
        CAMERA_PERMISSION_REQUEST_CODE -> {
            if (grantResults.isNotEmpty() && grantResults[0] == Package
Manager.PERMISSION_GRANTED) {
                // Permission granted; perform the required action.
            } else {
                // Permission denied; handle accordingly.
            }
        }
        // Handle other permission requests if needed.
    }
}
```

Checking Multiple Permissions

In some cases, your app may require multiple permissions to perform a specific task. You can request multiple permissions simultaneously and handle the responses accordingly.

```
val permissions = arrayOf(
    Manifest.permission.CAMERA,
    Manifest.permission.WRITE_EXTERNAL_STORAGE
)

val permissionResults = IntArray(permissions.size)

for (i in permissions.indices) {
    permissionResults[i] = ContextCompat.checkSelfPermission(this, permission
s[i])
}

if (permissionResults.all { it == PackageManager.PERMISSION_GRANTED }) {
    // All permissions are granted; proceed.
} else {
    // Request permissions for the ones that are not granted.
    ActivityCompat.requestPermissions(this, permissions, PERMISSIONS_REQUEST_
CODE)
}
```

Explaining Why Permissions Are Needed

It's essential to provide clear and concise explanations to users about why your app needs specific permissions. Android provides a built-in permission dialog that displays your explanation, but it's essential to set a rationale if the user has previously denied the permission request. You can use `shouldShowRequestPermissionRationale` to determine if a rationale is necessary:

```
if (ActivityCompat.shouldShowRequestPermissionRationale(this, Manifest.permis
sion.CAMERA)) {
    // Display a rationale to the user.
} else {
    // No need to show a rationale; request the permission directly.
    ActivityCompat.requestPermissions(this, arrayOf(Manifest.permission.CAMER
A), CAMERA_PERMISSION_REQUEST_CODE)
}
```

Handling Permission Denials

When a user denies a permission request, it's crucial to handle it gracefully. Provide alternative paths or functionality that doesn't require the denied permission. Additionally, you can guide users to the app's settings to manually enable the permission.

```
if (grantResults.isNotEmpty() && grantResults[0] == PackageManager.PERMISSION
_DENIED) {
    if (!ActivityCompat.shouldShowRequestPermissionRationale(this, Manifest.p
ermission.CAMERA)) {
        // Permission denied with "Never ask again" option; navigate to app s
ettings.
        val intent = Intent(Settings.ACTION_APPLICATION_DETAILS_SETTINGS)
        val uri = Uri.fromParts("package", packageName, null)
        intent.data = uri
        startActivity(intent)
    } else {
        // Permission denied; handle accordingly.
    }
}
```

Handling user permissions correctly not only ensures that your app functions as intended but also contributes to a positive user experience. Always prioritize user privacy and make sure your explanations for permission requests are transparent and concise.

Section 11.3: App Security Best Practices

App security is a paramount concern in Android development. Protecting user data and ensuring the integrity of your app is essential to building trust with your users. This section explores best practices for enhancing the security of your Android applications.

1. Use HTTPS for Network Communication

When your app communicates with remote servers, ensure that it uses secure HTTP (HTTPS) connections. HTTPS encrypts data transmitted between the app and the server, preventing eavesdropping and data tampering. Android provides libraries like OkHttp and libraries for implementing secure communication easily.

```
val client = OkHttpClient.Builder()
    .sslSocketFactory(sslSocketFactory, trustManager)
    .build()
```

2. Data Encryption

Sensitive data, such as user credentials and personal information, should be stored in an encrypted form. Android provides the Android Keystore for secure storage and encryption of keys and other confidential data.

```
val keystore = KeyStore.getInstance("AndroidKeyStore")
keystore.load(null)
val key = keystore.getKey("my_key", null)
```

3. Implement Authentication

Implement robust user authentication mechanisms to ensure that only authorized users can access certain features or data within your app. Use technologies like OAuth, OpenID Connect, or Firebase Authentication for secure user authentication.

```
// Firebase Authentication
FirebaseAuth.getInstance().signInWithEmailAndPassword(email, password)
```

4. Secure Code Practices

Follow secure coding practices to prevent common vulnerabilities like SQL injection, cross-site scripting (XSS), and code injection. Use parameterized queries for database access and validate user inputs to prevent malicious data input.

```
// SQL Injection Prevention
val query = "SELECT * FROM users WHERE username = ? AND password = ?"
db.rawQuery(query, arrayOf(username, password))
```

5. Regularly Update Dependencies

Keep your app's dependencies and libraries up to date. Security vulnerabilities can be patched in newer versions of libraries, so regularly check for updates and apply them to your project.

6. App Permissions

As discussed in the previous sections, request permissions appropriately and only access the data and device features necessary for your app's functionality. Limit unnecessary access to sensitive user data.

7. Code Obfuscation

Use code obfuscation techniques to make it harder for attackers to reverse engineer your app's code. ProGuard is a commonly used tool for code obfuscation in Android.

8. Regular Security Audits

Conduct regular security audits of your app's code and infrastructure. Vulnerabilities can evolve over time, so it's essential to stay vigilant and address any new threats promptly.

9. Implement a Secure Update Mechanism

Ensure that your app can receive security updates promptly. Implement a secure update mechanism that allows you to patch vulnerabilities without requiring users to download a new version from the app store.

10. User Education

Educate your users about best security practices within your app. Encourage them to use strong passwords, enable two-factor authentication, and be cautious about sharing personal information.

By incorporating these best practices into your Android app development process, you can significantly enhance its security and protect user data and privacy. Remember that security is an ongoing process, and staying informed about the latest security threats and mitigation techniques is essential.

Section 11.4: Data Encryption and Secure Storage

Data encryption is a crucial aspect of app security, especially when handling sensitive user information. This section discusses data encryption techniques and secure storage options available for Android app development.

1. Android Keystore

Android Keystore is a secure hardware-backed storage for cryptographic keys. It provides a secure environment for storing encryption keys, making it ideal for encrypting sensitive data like passwords, keys, and other confidential information.

```
// Initialize Android Keystore
val keyStore = KeyStore.getInstance("AndroidKeyStore")
keyStore.load(null)

// Generate a new key pair
val keyPairGenerator = KeyPairGenerator.getInstance(
    KeyProperties.KEY_ALGORITHM_RSA, "AndroidKeyStore"
)
val spec = KeyGenParameterSpec.Builder(
    alias,
    KeyProperties.PURPOSE_ENCRYPT or KeyProperties.PURPOSE_DECRYPT
).setBlockModes(KeyProperties.BLOCK_MODE_GCM)
    .setEncryptionPaddings(KeyProperties.ENCRYPTION_PADDING_RSA_PKCS1)
    .setRandomizedEncryptionRequired(false)
```

```
    .build()
keyPairGenerator.initialize(spec)
keyPairGenerator.generateKeyPair()
```

2. SharedPreferences

While SharedPreferences are often used for storing simple key-value pairs, it's essential to encrypt sensitive data before storing it in SharedPreferences. You can use Android Keystore to store encryption keys securely and use those keys to encrypt and decrypt data before storing it in SharedPreferences.

```
// Encrypt data before storing in SharedPreferences
val encryptedData = encryptData(dataToEncrypt, encryptionKey)

// Store encrypted data
val editor = sharedPreferences.edit()
editor.putString("encrypted_data", encryptedData)
editor.apply()
```

3. SQLCipher

If your app uses a local SQLite database, consider using SQLCipher, an open-source extension to SQLite that provides transparent 256-bit AES encryption for database files. It ensures that the data in your database remains secure even if the device is compromised.

```
implementation 'net.zetetic:android-database-sqlcipher:4.0.1'

// Initialize SQLCipher database
SQLiteDatabase.loadLibs(context)
val database = SQLiteDatabase.openOrCreateDatabase(
    databaseFile,
    password,
    null,
    null
)
```

4. File Encryption

When dealing with files or file-based storage, you can encrypt the files using encryption algorithms like AES. Ensure that you use strong encryption keys and securely manage them.

```
// Encrypt a file
val encryptedFile = FileEncryption.encrypt(fileToEncrypt, encryptionKey)

// Save the encrypted file
FileUtils.saveEncryptedFile(encryptedFile, destinationDirectory)
```

5. Network Data Encryption

When transmitting sensitive data over a network, use HTTPS to secure the communication between your app and the server. This ensures that data is encrypted during transit, protecting it from eavesdropping.

```
// Use HTTPS for network communication
val client = OkHttpClient.Builder()
    .sslSocketFactory(sslSocketFactory, trustManager)
    .build()
```

Data encryption and secure storage are critical components of app security. When implementing encryption, always follow best practices, securely manage encryption keys, and stay informed about the latest encryption standards and algorithms to keep your app's data safe from unauthorized access.

Section 11.5: OAuth and User Authentication

User authentication is a fundamental aspect of app security, ensuring that only authorized users can access certain features or data. OAuth is a widely used protocol for user authentication and authorization. In this section, we'll explore OAuth and its use in Android app development.

1. Understanding OAuth

OAuth (Open Authorization) is an open-standard protocol that allows applications to securely access resources on behalf of a user without exposing the user's credentials. It is commonly used for scenarios like social media logins, accessing cloud services, or authorizing third-party apps to interact with a user's data.

2. OAuth Flow

OAuth defines various authorization flows, but the most commonly used ones are the Authorization Code Flow and the Implicit Flow:

- **Authorization Code Flow:** In this flow, the app redirects the user to a login page (e.g., Google or Facebook). After the user logs in and grants permission, the app receives an authorization code, which it exchanges for an access token.

- **Implicit Flow:** In this flow, the app directly receives an access token after the user logs in and grants permission. It's typically used in single-page web apps and mobile apps.

3. OAuth Libraries

To implement OAuth in Android, you can use OAuth libraries such as AppAuth and Okta. These libraries simplify the OAuth flow and help you integrate third-party authentication providers seamlessly.

```
// Example dependency for AppAuth
implementation 'net.openid:appauth:0.7.1'
```

4. Google Sign-In

For integrating Google OAuth in your Android app, you can use the Google Sign-In API. It allows users to sign in with their Google accounts and provides access to various Google services.

```
implementation 'com.google.android.gms:play-services-auth:19.2.0'
```

5. Facebook Login

To implement OAuth using Facebook for user authentication, you can integrate the Facebook Login SDK. It allows users to log in with their Facebook credentials and access their Facebook data from your app.

```
implementation 'com.facebook.android:facebook-login:9.4.0'
```

6. Custom OAuth Providers

If your app uses a custom OAuth provider, you'll need to follow the provider's documentation to integrate OAuth. Typically, this involves registering your app with the provider, obtaining client credentials, and implementing the OAuth flow as specified.

7. Security Considerations

When implementing OAuth, it's crucial to follow security best practices. This includes securely storing OAuth tokens, using HTTPS for all communication, and regularly refreshing tokens. Additionally, stay informed about OAuth vulnerabilities and updates to ensure the security of your authentication mechanism.

OAuth is a powerful tool for user authentication and authorization in Android apps. By using OAuth libraries and following security best practices, you can provide a secure and user-friendly authentication experience for your app's users.

Chapter 12: Testing and Debugging

Debugging and testing are essential parts of the software development process. They help identify and fix issues in your code, ensuring that your app runs smoothly and meets its requirements. In this chapter, we'll explore various aspects of testing and debugging in Android app development.

Section 12.1: Unit Testing with Kotlin

Unit testing is the practice of testing individual units or components of your code in isolation to ensure they work correctly. In Android app development, unit tests are written to validate the behavior of specific functions or methods.

1. Why Unit Testing?

Unit testing provides several benefits:

- **Early Detection of Bugs:** Unit tests can catch bugs early in the development process, making it easier and cheaper to fix them.

- **Regression Testing:** Unit tests can be automated and run frequently to check if new code changes introduce regressions (unintended side effects).

- **Improved Code Quality:** Writing tests often leads to cleaner and more modular code, making it easier to maintain.

- **Documentation:** Unit tests serve as documentation for your code, showing how it's intended to be used.

2. Testing Frameworks

Android provides several testing frameworks for writing unit tests, with the most common ones being:

- **JUnit:** A widely-used framework for writing unit tests in Java and Kotlin.

- **Mockito:** A mocking framework that helps you create and configure mock objects for testing.

- **Espresso:** A testing framework for UI testing and UI automation.

3. Writing Unit Tests

Here's a basic example of writing a unit test in Kotlin using JUnit:

```
import org.junit.Test
import org.junit.Assert.*

class MyUnitTest {
```

```
@Test
fun addition_isCorrect() {
    assertEquals(4, 2 + 2)
}
}
```

In this example, we create a test class with a test method that asserts the result of a simple addition operation.

4. Running Unit Tests

You can run unit tests in Android Studio by right-clicking on the test class or method and selecting "Run."

5. Test-Driven Development (TDD)

Test-Driven Development is a methodology in which you write tests before writing the actual code. TDD can help you design your code with a clear focus on requirements and expected outcomes.

6. Continuous Integration (CI)

Integrating unit tests into your CI/CD pipeline ensures that tests are automatically run whenever changes are pushed to the code repository. Popular CI services like Jenkins, Travis CI, and CircleCI support Android app testing.

7. Best Practices
- Keep tests small and focused on one aspect of your code.
- Use meaningful test method and class names.
- Use mock objects to isolate the code under test from external dependencies.
- Aim for a high test coverage percentage to ensure comprehensive testing.

Unit testing with Kotlin and the appropriate testing frameworks can significantly improve the reliability and quality of your Android app. It's an essential practice for any serious Android developer and can save time and effort in the long run.

Section 12.2: Instrumented Testing

Instrumented testing, also known as UI testing or integration testing, is a critical aspect of Android app development. Unlike unit tests that focus on testing individual units of code in isolation, instrumented tests are designed to evaluate the behavior of your app as a whole, including how various components interact and how the app functions on a real device or emulator.

1. Why Instrumented Testing?

Instrumented testing offers several advantages:

- **Real-World Scenario Testing:** It allows you to simulate user interactions and real-world scenarios, ensuring your app behaves as expected in different situations.

- **UI Testing:** You can verify that the user interface elements (UI) of your app function correctly and that the user experience is smooth.

- **Device and Platform Compatibility:** Instrumented tests help you ensure that your app works on various Android devices and OS versions.

- **End-to-End Testing:** You can test complete user flows within your app, such as registration, login, and navigation between screens.

2. Android Testing Frameworks

Android provides two primary frameworks for writing instrumented tests:

- **Espresso:** Espresso is a popular testing framework for writing UI tests. It allows you to simulate user interactions like button clicks, text input, and gestures. Espresso is known for its simplicity and readability.

- **UI Automator:** UI Automator is another testing framework that provides a broader range of testing capabilities. It can interact with UI elements across multiple apps and perform more complex scenarios.

3. Writing Instrumented Tests

Here's an example of an instrumented test using Espresso to check if a login screen works correctly:

```
import androidx.test.ext.junit.rules.ActivityScenarioRule
import androidx.test.espresso.Espresso
import androidx.test.espresso.action.ViewActions
import androidx.test.espresso.assertion.ViewAssertions
import androidx.test.espresso.matcher.ViewMatchers
import org.junit.Rule
import org.junit.Test

class LoginActivityInstrumentedTest {

    @get:Rule
    val activityRule = ActivityScenarioRule(LoginActivity::class.java)

    @Test
    fun testLogin() {
        // Type text into username and password fields
        Espresso.onView(ViewMatchers.withId(R.id.editTextUsername)).perform(
            ViewActions.typeText("username")
```

```
    )
    Espresso.onView(ViewMatchers.withId(R.id.editTextPassword)).perform(
        ViewActions.typeText("password")
    )

    // Click the login button
    Espresso.onView(ViewMatchers.withId(R.id.buttonLogin)).perform(
        ViewActions.click()
    )

    // Check if the login was successful
    Espresso.onView(ViewMatchers.withId(R.id.textViewWelcome)).check(
        ViewAssertions.matches(ViewMatchers.isDisplayed())
    )
    }
}
```

In this example, we use Espresso to simulate typing text into username and password fields and clicking the login button. Finally, we check if the "Welcome" text view is displayed after a successful login.

4. Running Instrumented Tests

You can run instrumented tests in Android Studio by right-clicking on the test class or method and selecting "Run."

5. Continuous Integration (CI)

Similar to unit tests, it's crucial to integrate instrumented tests into your CI/CD pipeline. This ensures that your app is thoroughly tested on various devices and Android versions whenever changes are made to the codebase.

Instrumented testing is an essential part of app development, helping you identify and address issues related to the user interface, user interactions, and overall app functionality. By combining both unit and instrumented tests, you can ensure that your Android app is robust, reliable, and provides an excellent user experience.

Section 12.3: Debugging Techniques

Debugging is an integral part of the Android app development process. It involves identifying and resolving issues in your code to ensure that your app functions correctly and behaves as expected. This section will explore various debugging techniques and tools available for Android development.

1. Logging

Logging is one of the most fundamental debugging techniques. You can use the `Log` class in Android to print messages to the Android Monitor, which can be accessed through Android Studio. You can log various types of messages, such as information, warnings, and errors.

```kotlin
import android.util.Log

class MyActivity : AppCompatActivity() {
    override fun onCreate(savedInstanceState: Bundle?) {
        super.onCreate(savedInstanceState)
        setContentView(R.layout.activity_main)

        // Log an informational message
        Log.i("MyActivity", "Activity created")

        // Log a warning message
        Log.w("MyActivity", "This is a warning")

        // Log an error message
        Log.e("MyActivity", "An error occurred")
    }
}
```

2. Breakpoints

Android Studio provides a powerful debugging feature called breakpoints. You can set breakpoints in your code by clicking on the left margin of the code editor. When your app runs and reaches a breakpoint, it pauses execution, allowing you to inspect variables, step through code, and identify issues.

3. Android Profiler

The Android Profiler is a set of tools in Android Studio that helps you analyze your app's performance, memory usage, CPU usage, and more. It allows you to identify performance bottlenecks and memory leaks in your app.

4. Exception Handling

Proper exception handling is essential for robust Android apps. You can use try-catch blocks to catch exceptions and handle them gracefully. For example:

```kotlin
try {
    // Code that may throw an exception
    val result = divide(10, 0)
} catch (e: Exception) {
    // Handle the exception
    Log.e("MyActivity", "An error occurred: ${e.message}")
}
```

5. Remote Debugging

Android allows remote debugging, which means you can debug an app running on a physical device or emulator from your development machine. This is particularly useful when you need to debug issues that only occur in specific environments.

6. Profiling GPU Rendering

Android Studio provides tools to profile GPU rendering, helping you identify performance problems related to graphics rendering. This is crucial for apps that require smooth animations and transitions.

7. Debugging Libraries

There are several third-party debugging libraries available for Android development. One popular library is Stetho, which provides a debugging bridge for inspecting your app's database, shared preferences, and network traffic using Google Chrome's developer tools.

```
dependencies {
    implementation 'com.facebook.stetho:stetho:1.5.1'
}
```

8. Using Logcat

Logcat is a command-line tool that allows you to view logs generated by your app on an Android device or emulator. You can use it to monitor logs in real-time or filter logs based on specific criteria.

```
# View all log messages
adb logcat

# Filter logs by tag
adb logcat -s MyActivity
```

Debugging is a crucial skill for Android developers, and mastering these techniques and tools will help you diagnose and fix issues efficiently. Whether it's using logging, setting breakpoints, or utilizing Android Profiler, effective debugging will lead to more stable and reliable Android applications.

Section 12.4: Profiling and Performance Optimization

Profiling and performance optimization are essential steps in the development of Android applications. Profiling helps identify bottlenecks and performance issues, allowing you to create responsive and efficient apps. This section will cover various profiling techniques and tools available for Android development.

1. Android Profiler

Android Profiler is a powerful tool available in Android Studio that helps you analyze the performance of your app. It provides insights into CPU usage, memory allocation, network activity, and more. Here are some key features:

- **CPU Profiler**: Helps you identify methods that consume the most CPU time, allowing you to optimize code.
- **Memory Profiler**: Helps you track memory usage, find memory leaks, and optimize memory allocation.
- **Network Profiler**: Monitors network activity, including HTTP requests and responses, to optimize network operations.
- **Energy Profiler**: Measures battery usage, enabling you to optimize energy consumption.

2. Memory Optimization

Memory optimization is crucial to prevent your app from crashing due to memory-related issues. Use tools like the Memory Profiler to:

- Identify memory leaks by tracking object allocations and deallocations.
- Monitor memory usage over time to ensure efficient memory management.
- Analyze the impact of garbage collection on your app's performance.

3. CPU Optimization

To optimize CPU usage, you can use the CPU Profiler to:

- Identify performance bottlenecks in your code.
- Analyze thread activity and synchronization issues.
- Locate CPU-intensive methods and optimize them for better performance.

4. Network Optimization

For network optimization, the Network Profiler helps you:

- Monitor network requests and responses in real-time.
- Check for excessive network requests or large payloads.
- Identify slow or inefficient network operations and optimize them.

5. Method Tracing

Method tracing is a technique that records method execution times to identify slow or problematic functions. Android Profiler provides a method tracing feature that allows you to record method calls and analyze their performance.

```
Debug.startMethodTracing("my_trace_file")
// Code to be profiled
Debug.stopMethodTracing()
```

6. Systrace

Systrace is a tool that provides a detailed timeline of system events, including CPU usage, UI rendering, and other system activities. It helps you understand how your app interacts with the system and identify performance bottlenecks.

```
$ adb shell
$ systrace -a com.example.myapp -b 10000 -t 5
```

7. Third-Party Profiling Libraries

There are third-party libraries available for profiling and performance optimization, such as LeakCanary for memory leak detection and Performance-Tools for CPU profiling. These libraries can be integrated into your app to streamline the profiling process.

8. Regular Testing and Profiling

Profiling and performance optimization should be ongoing processes throughout your app's development. Regularly test your app on different devices and Android versions to ensure consistent performance.

By employing profiling techniques and using tools like Android Profiler, you can enhance the performance and responsiveness of your Android applications. Identifying and resolving performance bottlenecks and memory issues will result in a better user experience and higher user satisfaction.

Section 12.5: Continuous Integration and Deployment

Continuous Integration (CI) and Continuous Deployment (CD) are essential practices in modern software development. They help automate and streamline the process of building, testing, and deploying Android applications. In this section, we will explore how to set up CI/CD pipelines for Android development.

1. Benefits of CI/CD for Android

CI/CD offers several benefits for Android app development:

- **Automation**: Automated builds and tests reduce manual work, ensuring consistent and error-free deployments.
- **Faster Releases**: CI/CD pipelines accelerate the release process, allowing you to deliver updates to users more quickly.
- **Quality Assurance**: Automated testing helps catch bugs early in the development cycle.
- **Stability**: CD pipelines enable frequent deployments with minimal downtime.

2. Setting Up CI/CD Pipelines

2.1. Version Control

Start by using a version control system (e.g., Git) to manage your Android project. Host your repository on platforms like GitHub, GitLab, or Bitbucket.

2.2. Build Automation

Use build automation tools like Gradle to define and automate your build process. Gradle scripts can compile code, package your app, and generate APK files.

2.3. Continuous Integration

Choose a CI platform like Jenkins, Travis CI, CircleCI, or GitHub Actions to set up CI pipelines. These platforms can automatically build and test your app whenever changes are pushed to the repository.

Here's a simplified example of a GitHub Actions workflow for Android:

```yaml
name: Build and Test

on:
  push:
    branches:
      - main

jobs:
  build:
    runs-on: ubuntu-latest

    steps:
      - name: Checkout code
        uses: actions/checkout@v2

      - name: Set up JDK
        uses: actions/setup-java@v2
        with:
          java-version: '11'

      - name: Build with Gradle
        run: ./gradlew build

      - name: Run Tests
        run: ./gradlew test
```

For CD, consider platforms like Google Play Console for production releases and Firebase App Distribution for internal testing. Configure deployment pipelines to automatically publish your app to the Google Play Store or distribute it to testers.

3. Automated Testing

In CI/CD, automated testing is crucial. Write unit tests, UI tests, and integration tests to ensure the quality and stability of your app. CI platforms can run these tests automatically on each code commit.

4. Code Quality and Code Review

Integrate code quality tools like Lint and Detekt to ensure code adherence to best practices. Implement code review processes to maintain code quality standards.

5. Monitoring and Rollbacks

Set up monitoring and crash reporting tools like Firebase Crashlytics or Sentry to track app performance in production. In case of issues, implement rollback mechanisms to revert to a stable version.

6. Gradual Rollouts and Feature Flags

To minimize risk, use gradual rollouts on the Google Play Store to release updates to a small percentage of users initially. Feature flags allow you to enable or disable specific features remotely, providing control over app behavior.

7. Security Considerations

In CI/CD, pay attention to security. Implement security scanning tools to identify vulnerabilities in your app and dependencies. Store sensitive credentials securely using secrets management tools provided by CI platforms.

8. Documentation

Document your CI/CD pipeline setup, including build scripts, deployment configurations, and testing procedures. This documentation is valuable for your development team and future maintainers.

By implementing CI/CD practices in your Android development workflow, you can enhance productivity, maintain code quality, and deliver a more reliable and responsive app to your users. CI/CD pipelines ensure that your app is continuously tested and deployed, reducing the risk of errors and improving the overall development process.

Chapter 13: Building Robust Apps

Robustness is a critical aspect of Android app development. It refers to an app's ability to perform well under various conditions, handle errors gracefully, and recover from unexpected situations. In this chapter, we'll explore techniques and best practices for building robust Android apps.

Section 13.1: Error Handling and Crash Reporting

Effective error handling and crash reporting are fundamental to building a robust Android app. Users expect apps to work without unexpected crashes or errors. Here's how you can improve error handling and crash reporting in your app:

1. Crash Reporting Tools

- Utilize crash reporting tools like Firebase Crashlytics, Sentry, or Bugsnag. These tools automatically collect crash reports and provide insights into the root causes of crashes.

2. Logcat and Logging

- Use Android's Logcat system for logging. Implement logging at different levels (verbose, debug, info, warning, error) to capture relevant information.

```java
Log.d(TAG, "This is a debug message");
Log.e(TAG, "This is an error message", exception);
```

3. Try-Catch Blocks

- Wrap potentially problematic code in try-catch blocks to prevent crashes. Handle exceptions gracefully by displaying user-friendly error messages or logging the issue.

```java
try {
    // Risky code here
} catch (Exception e) {
    Log.e(TAG, "An error occurred", e);
    // Display an error message to the user
}
```

4. Default Error Handlers

- Android provides a default uncaught exception handler. Override this handler to perform custom actions, like sending error reports.

```java
Thread.setDefaultUncaughtExceptionHandler(new Thread.UncaughtExceptionHandler
() {
    @Override
    public void uncaughtException(Thread t, Throwable e) {
        // Handle the uncaught exception
    }
});
```

5. Feedback Mechanism

- Include a feedback mechanism in your app, allowing users to report issues. Capture additional information such as device details and app version to assist with troubleshooting.

6. Testing for Exceptions

- Create test cases that intentionally trigger exceptions to ensure your error-handling mechanisms work as expected.

7. Release Error-Free Updates

- Prioritize fixing reported crashes in your app updates. Regularly review crash reports and address the most critical issues.

8. User-Friendly Error Messages

- When displaying error messages to users, make them informative and actionable. Clearly explain the issue and suggest steps to resolve it.

9. Analyze Crash Reports

- Regularly review crash reports to identify patterns and common causes of crashes. Use this data to prioritize bug fixes.

10. Automated Testing

- Implement automated testing, including unit tests and UI tests, to catch potential issues before they reach users.

Building a robust Android app involves a proactive approach to error handling and continuous improvement. By using crash reporting tools, logging, try-catch blocks, and a robust error-handling strategy, you can provide users with a more reliable and stable app experience. Remember to analyze crash reports and actively address issues to ensure your app's long-term success.

Section 13.2: Memory Management and Optimization

Memory management is a critical aspect of building robust Android apps. In this section, we'll explore techniques for effective memory management and optimization to ensure your app performs well and doesn't consume excessive system resources.

Understanding Android Memory Management

Android apps run within a constrained environment, with limited memory resources available. To optimize memory usage, it's essential to understand how Android manages memory:

- **Heap Memory:** Android uses a managed heap memory for storing objects created by your app. The heap is divided into two main regions: the Java heap for Java objects and the native heap for native code objects.

- **Garbage Collection:** Android's garbage collector automatically reclaims memory occupied by objects that are no longer in use. Frequent garbage collection can lead to performance issues, so minimizing unnecessary object creation is crucial.

Memory Optimization Techniques

Here are some memory optimization techniques for your Android app:

1. Use Memory Profiling Tools
- Android Studio provides memory profiling tools to analyze your app's memory usage. These tools can help identify memory leaks, high memory usage, and inefficient memory allocations.

2. Avoid Memory Leaks
- Memory leaks occur when objects that are no longer needed still hold references, preventing them from being garbage collected. Common causes of memory leaks include static references and improper context usage. Use tools like LeakCanary to detect memory leaks early in development.

3. Optimize Bitmaps
- Bitmaps can consume significant memory, especially when loading large images. Use techniques like downsampling and caching to reduce memory usage when working with bitmaps.

4. Release Resources
- Explicitly release resources when they are no longer needed. For example, close database connections, release file handles, and unregister event listeners.

5. Load Data Efficiently
- When working with data, load only the data you need, and release it when you're done. Consider using pagination and lazy loading for large data sets.

6. Reduce Object Creation
- Minimize object creation, especially in performance-critical code paths. Reuse objects whenever possible, and be mindful of auto-boxing when dealing with primitive types.

7. Use the Android Profiler
- The Android Profiler in Android Studio provides real-time monitoring of CPU, memory, and network usage. Use it to identify performance bottlenecks and memory issues during app development.

8. Implement a Cache Strategy
- Implement a caching mechanism for frequently used data to reduce the need for repeated data retrieval, which can be resource-intensive.

9. Choose Data Structures Wisely

- Select data structures that are efficient in terms of memory usage and access times. For example, use SparseArray instead of HashMap when working with integer keys.

10. Optimize Image Loading

- Use libraries like Picasso or Glide for image loading, as they offer image caching, resizing, and memory optimization out of the box.

11. Test on Low-End Devices

- Test your app on low-end devices with limited memory to ensure it performs well across a range of hardware.

12. Implement OnTrimMemory

- Use the `onTrimMemory()` method to release resources and reduce memory usage when your app goes into the background or the system is under memory pressure.

Effective memory management and optimization are essential for creating Android apps that provide a smooth user experience. Regularly profile and analyze your app's memory usage, address memory leaks, and apply optimization techniques to minimize resource consumption. By doing so, you'll ensure that your app performs well on a variety of Android devices and maintains a good reputation among users.

Section 13.3: App Lifecycle and State Management

Understanding the Android app lifecycle and effectively managing the state of your app is crucial for building robust and responsive applications. In this section, we'll dive into the Android app lifecycle and explore best practices for state management.

Android App Lifecycle

Android apps go through various states during their lifecycle. It's essential to grasp these states to manage your app's behavior correctly:

1. **Not Running:** The app has been terminated or has not yet been started.
2. **Inactive:** The app is running but not in focus and can be paused or stopped at any time.
3. **Active:** The app is running and in the foreground.
4. **Background:** The app is no longer visible but still running.
5. **Terminated:** The app has been terminated or removed from memory.

Android provides several lifecycle methods that allow you to respond to these state transitions, such as onCreate(), onStart(), onResume(), onPause(), onStop(), and onDestroy().

State Management Best Practices

Here are some best practices for managing the state of your Android app effectively:

1. Use onSaveInstanceState() and onRestoreInstanceState():
- These methods allow you to save and restore crucial data when your app undergoes configuration changes, like screen rotations. Use them to persist user data and ensure a smooth user experience.

```
@Override
protected void onSaveInstanceState(Bundle outState) {
    super.onSaveInstanceState(outState);
    outState.putString("key", value);
}


@Override
protected void onRestoreInstanceState(Bundle savedInstanceState) {
    super.onRestoreInstanceState(savedInstanceState);
    value = savedInstanceState.getString("key");
}
```

2. ViewModel for UI-Related Data:
- Use the `ViewModel` class to store and manage UI-related data. ViewModels survive configuration changes and allow you to separate UI logic from the underlying data.

```
public class MyViewModel extends ViewModel {
    private MutableLiveData<String> data = new MutableLiveData<>();

    public void setData(String value) {
        data.setValue(value);
    }

    public LiveData<String> getData() {
        return data;
    }
}
```

3. Save Data to SharedPreferences:
- Use `SharedPreferences` to store simple key-value pairs persistently. This is suitable for settings and user preferences.

```
SharedPreferences preferences = getSharedPreferences("MyPrefs", MODE_PRIVATE);
SharedPreferences.Editor editor = preferences.edit();
editor.putString("key", value);
editor.apply();
```

4. Database for Structured Data:
- If your app handles structured data, use a local database (e.g., Room) to store and manage it. This ensures data persistence and enables efficient querying.

- When performing background tasks, consider using background services or WorkManager to ensure tasks are completed even if the app goes into the background.

6. *Use LiveData for Data Observation:*

- LiveData allows you to observe data changes and automatically update UI components when the underlying data changes. It's especially useful when working with databases or remote data sources.

7. *Handle Lifecycle-Aware Components:*

- Use LifecycleObserver and LiveData to make your components aware of the app's lifecycle. This ensures that resources are released appropriately.

8. *Release Resources in onDestroy():*

- Ensure that you release resources like database connections, file handles, and event listeners in the onDestroy() method to avoid memory leaks.

Effective state management in Android apps involves careful consideration of the app's lifecycle and the appropriate use of tools and patterns like ViewModel, SharedPreferences, LiveData, and background processing mechanisms. By following these best practices, you can build apps that provide a seamless user experience while maintaining data integrity across various device configurations and states.

Section 13.4: Handling Configuration Changes

Handling configuration changes, such as screen rotations or language changes, is an essential aspect of building a responsive Android app. This section explores the challenges posed by configuration changes and provides strategies to manage them effectively.

Understanding Configuration Changes

Configuration changes occur when the device's configuration, like screen orientation, locale, or font size, changes. By default, Android destroys and recreates the activity during configuration changes, which can lead to data loss and a poor user experience.

Common configuration changes include: - **Screen Rotation:** Switching between portrait and landscape modes. - **Locale Change:** Switching the device's language or region. - **Font Size Change:** Adjusting the system's font size.

Challenges of Configuration Changes

The primary challenge posed by configuration changes is the loss of activity state. For example, if a user enters data into a form, rotates the device, and the activity is recreated, the entered data is lost. To address this, you need to implement strategies to preserve and restore critical data.

Handling Configuration Changes

Here are strategies to handle configuration changes gracefully:

1. Use onSaveInstanceState() and onRestoreInstanceState():
- Implement these methods to save and restore critical data, such as user input, in the Bundle object.

```
@Override
protected void onSaveInstanceState(Bundle outState) {
    super.onSaveInstanceState(outState);
    outState.putString("key", value);
}


@Override
protected void onRestoreInstanceState(Bundle savedInstanceState) {
    super.onRestoreInstanceState(savedInstanceState);
    value = savedInstanceState.getString("key");
}
```

2. Prevent Activity Recreation:
- You can prevent the activity from being recreated during configuration changes by adding android:configChanges to your activity's manifest entry.

```
<activity
    android:name=".MyActivity"
    android:configChanges="orientation|screenSize|locale">
    <!-- Other activity attributes -->
</activity>
```

This approach requires manually handling configuration changes by overriding onConfigurationChanged().

```
@Override
public void onConfigurationChanged(Configuration newConfig) {
    super.onConfigurationChanged(newConfig);
    // Handle configuration changes here
}
```

3. ViewModel for UI-Related Data:
- Use Android's ViewModel class to store UI-related data. ViewModels survive configuration changes and prevent data loss.

```
public class MyViewModel extends ViewModel {
    private MutableLiveData<String> data = new MutableLiveData<>();

    public void setData(String value) {
        data.setValue(value);
    }

    public LiveData<String> getData() {
        return data;
```

```
        }
}
```

4. Use Fragments:

- Fragments are more flexible than activities in handling configuration changes. Consider using fragments to separate UI components, as they can be retained during configuration changes.

5. Handle Resources Dynamically:

- Instead of hardcoding resources like strings or layouts, retrieve them dynamically based on the current configuration using resource qualifiers (e.g., `res/values` and `res/values-fr`).

6. Test Configuration Changes:

- Ensure that your app functions correctly after configuration changes by testing it thoroughly, including screen rotations and locale changes.

7. Persist Data When Necessary:

- For data that should survive configuration changes, consider persisting it in a local database or SharedPreferences.

Handling configuration changes effectively is crucial for creating a seamless user experience in your Android app. By using the recommended techniques and considering the user's data and context, you can ensure that your app remains responsive and user-friendly even when the device's configuration changes.

Section 13.5: App Compatibility and Support Libraries

Ensuring that your Android app is compatible with various devices and Android versions is crucial for reaching a broad audience and providing a consistent user experience. This section discusses app compatibility and the use of support libraries to address compatibility challenges.

Understanding App Compatibility

App compatibility refers to an app's ability to run correctly and provide a good user experience across a wide range of Android devices with varying hardware capabilities and screen sizes. It also involves ensuring that your app remains functional on different Android versions, as not all users will have the latest OS.

Challenges in App Compatibility

1. **Device Fragmentation:** The Android ecosystem has a wide variety of devices with different screen sizes, resolutions, and hardware capabilities. Ensuring your app looks and works well on all of them can be challenging.

2. **Android Version Compatibility:** New Android versions introduce changes and features. Supporting older versions while making use of the latest features requires careful planning.

3. **Screen Orientation and Form Factors:** Supporting both portrait and landscape modes and adapting to different form factors, such as tablets and foldable phones, is essential.

Strategies for App Compatibility

1. Responsive Design:
- Use responsive layouts and adaptive UI components to ensure your app looks good on various screen sizes and orientations. Techniques like ConstraintLayout can help create flexible UIs.

2. AndroidX Libraries:
- AndroidX is a set of libraries that provides backward-compatible versions of Android framework components. It allows you to use modern features on older devices. For example, using `androidx.appcompat` for modern app bars.

3. Material Design:
- Follow Material Design guidelines for UI components to ensure a consistent and visually appealing user interface across devices. Material Design provides a unified design language.

4. Compatibility Testing:
- Test your app on a range of physical and virtual devices to identify and fix compatibility issues. Use tools like Android Virtual Device Manager (AVD Manager) to create virtual devices for testing.

5. Minimum SDK Version:
- Set a reasonable minimum SDK version that supports the features your app needs. This ensures compatibility with older devices.

6. Feature Detection:
- Use feature detection to determine if a device supports specific features or hardware before attempting to use them. This prevents crashes on unsupported devices.

7. Dynamic Delivery:
- Use Android's App Bundle format to deliver optimized APKs to different devices. This reduces the size of your app for users and ensures they get the appropriate resources for their device.

8. Regular Updates:
- Keep your app up-to-date with the latest Android features and security patches. This encourages users to trust and continue using your app.

9. User Feedback:

- Encourage users to provide feedback about compatibility issues. This helps you identify and address problems specific to certain devices or configurations.

Ensuring app compatibility is an ongoing process that involves continuous testing and adaptation. By following these strategies and staying informed about changes in the Android ecosystem, you can provide a great user experience to a wide range of Android users.

Chapter 14: Creating Wearable and IoT Apps

Wearable devices and the Internet of Things (IoT) have gained significant popularity, offering new opportunities for Android app developers. In this chapter, we'll explore the world of wearables and IoT and how to create apps for these platforms.

Section 14.1: Introduction to Wearable Devices

Wearable devices are small electronic gadgets that can be worn on the body, often designed to serve specific purposes and provide convenience and accessibility. These devices have evolved from simple fitness trackers to powerful, multifunctional devices that can run apps. Some popular wearable platforms include Wear OS by Google (formerly Android Wear), Apple Watch, and fitness trackers like Fitbit.

Types of Wearable Devices

1. **Smartwatches:** Smartwatches are perhaps the most recognizable type of wearable. They can display notifications, track health and fitness data, and run apps.

2. **Fitness Trackers:** These devices focus on health and activity tracking. They monitor steps, heart rate, sleep patterns, and more.

3. **Augmented Reality (AR) Glasses:** AR glasses overlay digital information onto the wearer's view of the real world, enabling immersive experiences.

4. **Hearable Devices:** These include smart headphones and earbuds with additional features like voice assistants and fitness tracking.

Developing for Wearable Devices

Developing apps for wearables often involves using specialized SDKs and design considerations. Here are some key points to keep in mind:

- **SDKs:** Each wearable platform typically provides its SDK (e.g., Wear OS for Android wearables, watchOS for Apple Watch). These SDKs allow you to create apps specifically tailored to the device's form factor and capabilities.

- **User Interface:** Wearable screens are much smaller than those of smartphones or tablets. Designing a clear and concise user interface is crucial for usability.

- **Battery Efficiency:** Wearable devices have limited battery life. Ensure that your app is optimized for power consumption.

- **Health and Fitness:** If your app involves health and fitness tracking, make use of sensors like heart rate monitors and accelerometers.

- **Notifications:** Wearables excel at delivering timely notifications. Use this capability to enhance the user experience.

- **Voice Input:** Many wearables support voice commands. Integrating voice input can make your app more user-friendly.

- **Testing:** Testing on actual devices is essential due to the unique nature of wearables. Consider factors like touch gestures and screen size.

Wearable technology is continually evolving, and developers have the opportunity to create innovative apps that enhance users' lives in various ways. Whether you're interested in fitness, productivity, or augmented reality, this chapter will provide insights into building apps for wearable devices.

Section 14.2: Developing for Wear OS

Wear OS by Google, formerly known as Android Wear, is a platform specifically designed for smartwatches and wearables. Developing apps for Wear OS allows you to extend the functionality of Android devices to the wrist, providing users with convenient access to information and services. In this section, we'll explore the basics of developing apps for Wear OS.

Setting Up Your Development Environment

Before you can start developing for Wear OS, you need to set up your development environment. Here are the steps to get started:

1. **Install Android Studio:** Android Studio is the official integrated development environment (IDE) for Android app development. You can download it from the Android Studio website.

2. **Install the Android Wear Component:** Android Studio includes tools for Wear OS development. During the installation process, make sure to select the "Android Wear" component to enable Wear OS development support.

3. **Configure an Emulator or Use a Physical Device:** You can test your Wear OS apps on a physical Wear OS device or use the Wear OS emulator provided by Android Studio. To set up a Wear OS emulator, open the "AVD Manager" in Android Studio and create a new Wear OS Virtual Device.

Designing for the Wrist

Wear OS apps have a unique design challenge due to the limited screen size of smartwatches. Here are some design considerations:

- **Card-Based UI:** Wear OS apps often use a card-based user interface to present information and actions. Cards are easy to scroll through and interact with on a small screen.

- **Voice Input:** Wear OS devices support voice input, so consider integrating voice commands into your app to make it more user-friendly.

- **Glanceable Information:** Users often check their smartwatches for quick, glanceable information. Design your app to provide essential data at a glance.

Developing for Wear OS

Wear OS apps are essentially Android apps, but they have unique considerations:

- **Permissions:** Declare permissions carefully. Some permissions may not make sense for a wearable app, and unnecessary permissions can impact user trust.

- **App Architecture:** Consider using a modular architecture like MVVM (Model-View-ViewModel) to separate concerns and make your code more maintainable.

- **Notifications:** Take advantage of the rich notification system on Wear OS. You can create custom notifications and actions for your app.

- **Data Sync:** Ensure that your app can sync data between the wearable and the paired smartphone. Wear OS devices are often used in conjunction with smartphones.

Testing and Debugging

Testing Wear OS apps is crucial, and you can use both emulators and physical devices for testing. Debugging can be done using Android Studio's debugging tools.

Distributing Your Wear OS App

To distribute your Wear OS app, you can publish it on the Google Play Store alongside its companion Android app. Users can install the Wear OS app directly from their smartwatches or using the paired smartphone.

Developing for Wear OS opens up exciting possibilities for creating innovative apps that enhance users' wearable experiences. Whether it's delivering notifications, fitness tracking, or unique watch faces, Wear OS provides a versatile platform for developers.

Section 14.3: IoT Integration with Android Things

Android Things was Google's platform for building IoT (Internet of Things) devices using the Android operating system. However, Google officially deprecated Android Things in 2019, and it is no longer actively developed. Despite this, it's worth exploring what Android Things was and how it related to IoT development.

Android Things was an Android-based platform designed for IoT devices. It allowed developers to build smart, connected products using Android as the underlying operating system. Android Things provided many of the familiar Android development tools and APIs, making it easier for Android developers to venture into IoT development.

1. **Support for Common Hardware Platforms:** Android Things supported a variety of hardware platforms, including the Raspberry Pi, Intel Edison, and NXP Pico.

2. **Developer-Friendly Tools:** Developers could use Android Studio, the official Android development IDE, to create Android Things applications. This made it easier for Android developers to transition to IoT development.

3. **Integration with Google Services:** Android Things integrated with Google Cloud Platform services, enabling cloud-based processing and data storage for IoT applications.

Google deprecated Android Things because it decided to shift its focus away from the IoT platform. Instead, Google recommended using other IoT platforms and technologies, such as Google Cloud IoT Core and Android's built-in support for IoT features.

If you're interested in IoT development on Android, you can explore the following alternatives:

1. **Android for IoT:** Android provides built-in support for many IoT features, including Bluetooth connectivity, Wi-Fi support, and sensor integration. You can develop Android apps that run on IoT devices using the Android framework.

2. **Google Cloud IoT:** Google Cloud offers a comprehensive set of IoT services, including data ingestion, storage, and analytics. You can build IoT solutions that leverage Google Cloud's capabilities for data processing and machine learning.

3. **IoT Platforms:** There are numerous IoT platforms and frameworks available, such as Arduino, Raspberry Pi, and Particle. These platforms provide hardware and software tools for building IoT applications.

4. **Embedded Systems Development:** If you're interested in lower-level IoT development, you can explore embedded systems programming using languages like C and C++. This allows for precise control over hardware but typically involves a steeper learning curve.

In summary, while Android Things was a promising platform for IoT development, its deprecation means that developers should explore other options for building IoT applications. Android itself provides robust support for IoT features, and there are various IoT platforms and frameworks available to suit different project requirements.

Section 14.4: Wearable UI Design

Designing user interfaces (UI) for wearable devices presents unique challenges and opportunities compared to traditional mobile or desktop UI design. Wearable devices, such as smartwatches and fitness trackers, have limited screen real estate and are often used in situations where users need quick and convenient access to information. In this section, we'll explore the principles and best practices for designing effective UIs for wearable devices.

Key Considerations for Wearable UI Design

1. Keep It Simple:
- Due to the small screen size of wearables, simplicity is key. Focus on displaying only essential information and actions to avoid overwhelming users.

2. Glanceable Information:
- Design UIs that allow users to quickly "glance" at the screen and obtain the information they need within seconds. Use concise text, icons, and visual cues.

3. Context Awareness:
- Leverage sensors and context-awareness to tailor UI content. For example, display fitness stats during a workout and notifications during the day.

4. Minimal Interaction:
- Minimize the need for user input. Use gestures, voice commands, or simple taps for interaction. Avoid complex touch gestures.

5. Consistency Across Devices:
- If your app runs on multiple wearable devices, ensure a consistent UI and user experience across platforms.

6. Voice Commands:
- Integrate voice commands where appropriate. Many wearables support voice input, which can be a convenient way to interact with apps.

7. Battery Efficiency:
- Optimize your UI for battery life. Avoid animations and continuous background processes that can drain the device's battery quickly.

Designing for Smartwatches vs. Fitness Trackers

Smartwatches:

- Smartwatches often have color screens and support more complex UI elements. You can design watch faces, interactive notifications, and apps with richer visuals.

Fitness Trackers:

- Fitness trackers usually have monochrome screens and are primarily focused on health and fitness data. The UI is typically more straightforward, with a focus on displaying activity stats.

Prototyping and Testing

Before finalizing your wearable UI design, create prototypes and conduct usability testing. Prototyping tools and wearable simulators can help you visualize and refine your design. Usability testing with real users will provide valuable insights into the effectiveness of your UI.

Developer Tools

Most wearable platforms provide SDKs and design guidelines to assist developers in creating user-friendly interfaces. Familiarize yourself with these resources to make the most of the platform's capabilities.

Conclusion

Designing for wearables requires a shift in mindset compared to designing for other devices. Prioritize simplicity, glanceable information, and context awareness to create UIs that enhance the user experience on wearable devices. Additionally, stay updated with the latest developments in wearable technology and design trends to create compelling and relevant user interfaces.

Section 14.5: Voice Input and Assistant Integration

Voice input and virtual assistant integration play a significant role in the usability and functionality of wearable devices. They enable users to interact with their devices in a natural and convenient way, especially when the small form factor makes traditional input methods less practical. In this section, we'll explore how voice input and virtual assistant integration are utilized in wearable apps and devices.

Voice Input for Wearables

1. **Voice Commands**: Many wearable devices, including smartwatches, support voice commands. Users can trigger actions or retrieve information by speaking commands aloud. For example, a user can say, "Show my heart rate" to get their current heart rate data.

2. **Voice Text Input**: Some wearables also support voice-to-text input. Users can dictate messages, set reminders, or perform web searches by speaking into the device's microphone.

3. **Voice Search**: Voice search is a common feature on smartwatches and other wearables. Users can initiate web searches or search for content within apps using their voice.

4. **Voice Feedback**: Wearables can provide voice feedback in response to user actions. For instance, when a user completes a workout, the wearable may congratulate them with a spoken message.

Virtual Assistant Integration

1. **Voice Assistants**: Virtual voice assistants like Google Assistant, Siri, and Amazon Alexa are often integrated into wearables. Users can ask these assistants questions, control smart home devices, or perform various tasks via voice commands.

2. **Notifications**: Wearables can display notifications from virtual assistants. Users can receive weather updates, news briefings, and appointment reminders through their wearable device.

3. **Contextual Assistance**: Wearables leverage contextual information to provide more relevant assistance. For example, a user can ask their wearable, "What's my next appointment?" and receive the answer based on their calendar data.

Developing for Voice Input and Virtual Assistants

When developing for wearables with voice input and virtual assistant integration, consider the following:

1. **Voice Recognition**: *Utilize voice recognition APIs provided by the platform to accurately process voice commands and convert speech to text.*

2. **Natural Language Processing**: *Make use of natural language processing (NLP) to understand user queries better and provide more context-aware responses.*

3. **Privacy and Security**: *Be mindful of user privacy and data security, especially when handling voice data. Ensure that user data is protected and handled in compliance with privacy regulations.*

4. **User Experience**: *Focus on delivering a seamless and intuitive voice experience. Provide clear voice feedback and ensure that voice commands are responsive.*

5. **Testing**: *Thoroughly test voice commands and virtual assistant interactions to identify and address any issues or usability challenges.*

Conclusion

Voice input and virtual assistant integration enhance the usability and versatility of wearable devices. By providing users with the ability to interact with their wearables via voice, developers can create more user-friendly and efficient wearable apps. As voice technology continues to advance, integrating these features into wearable applications will become increasingly important for delivering a superior user experience.

Chapter 15: Publishing and Distribution

Section 15.1: Preparing Your App for Release

When you've completed developing your Android app, the next crucial step is preparing it for release. This process involves several tasks to ensure that your app is ready for distribution to users through the Google Play Store or other app distribution platforms. In this section, we'll walk through the essential steps to prepare your app for release.

1. Code Review and Testing

Before releasing your app, conduct a thorough code review and testing process. Ensure that your code is clean, free from bugs, and follows best practices. Test your app on various devices and Android versions to identify and fix any compatibility issues. Additionally, perform functional testing to verify that all app features work as intended.

2. Performance Optimization

Optimize your app's performance to provide a smooth user experience. Address issues related to app speed, responsiveness, and memory usage. Profiling tools like Android Studio's Profiler can help you identify bottlenecks and optimize your code. Pay attention to memory management to prevent memory leaks.

3. Security Review

Review your app's security measures to protect user data and privacy. Ensure that you're not storing sensitive information in plain text and that you're using secure communication protocols for network requests. Implement proper authentication and authorization mechanisms to safeguard user accounts.

4. Localization and Internationalization

If your app targets a global audience, consider localization and internationalization. Provide translations for different languages and adapt your app's content and layout to accommodate various regions and cultures. This makes your app more accessible and user-friendly to a broader audience.

5. Accessibility Testing

Conduct accessibility testing to ensure that your app is usable by individuals with disabilities. Android provides accessibility features, and it's essential to make your app compatible with these features. Test screen readers, keyboard navigation, and other accessibility tools to identify and fix any issues.

6. Compliance with Store Policies

Familiarize yourself with the policies and guidelines of the app store where you intend to publish your app, such as the Google Play Store. Ensure that your app complies with these policies, including content restrictions, monetization rules, and user data handling. Non-compliance can lead to rejection or removal from the store.

7. User Documentation

Prepare user documentation or help resources for your app. This may include an app description, privacy policy, terms of service, and user guides. Providing clear and informative documentation helps users understand your app and its features.

8. Version Management

Decide on a version number for your app and update the version code and name in your project. Version management is crucial for tracking app updates and ensuring that users receive the latest improvements and bug fixes.

9. Build Variants

Configure different build variants for your app, such as debug and release builds. The release build should have optimizations enabled and debugging information removed. Ensure that you're signing the release build with the appropriate keystore to prove the app's authenticity.

10. Generate a Signed APK

To distribute your app, you'll need to generate a signed APK (Android Package). Android Studio provides a wizard to guide you through this process. Sign the APK with your keystore to establish the app's identity and integrity.

11. Proguard or R8

Consider using Proguard or R8 for code obfuscation and shrinking. These tools can reduce the size of your APK and make it more challenging for attackers to reverse-engineer your code.

12. Beta Testing

Before a full release, consider conducting beta testing to gather feedback from a limited group of users. Beta testers can help identify issues and provide valuable insights. Google Play provides features for beta testing and staged rollouts.

13. Prepare Marketing Materials

Prepare marketing materials, such as app screenshots, promotional images, and a compelling app description. These assets are crucial for attracting users on app stores.

Once you've completed these steps, your app is well-prepared for release. In the next sections, we'll explore the process of submitting your app to the Google Play Store and handling the distribution and maintenance phases.

Section 15.2: Google Play Store Submission

After you've thoroughly prepared your Android app for release, the next step is to submit it to the Google Play Store, one of the most popular app distribution platforms for Android. This section will guide you through the process of submitting your app to the Play Store and making it available to users worldwide.

1. Google Play Developer Console

To begin, you'll need a developer account on the Google Play Developer Console. If you haven't already, sign up for a developer account and pay the one-time registration fee. You can use your Google account for this purpose.

2. Create a New App Listing

In the Google Play Developer Console, create a new app listing for your Android app. You'll need to provide various details about your app, including its title, description, icon, screenshots, and promotional graphics. Make sure to follow the Play Store's guidelines for creating appealing and informative listings.

3. Pricing and Distribution

Set the pricing and distribution settings for your app. Decide whether your app will be free or paid, and choose the countries or regions where you want to make it available. You can also select whether to offer in-app purchases and subscriptions.

4. Content Rating

Complete the content rating questionnaire to determine the appropriate content rating for your app. The Play Store uses this rating to inform users about the app's content and suitability for different age groups.

5. App Release

Prepare your app for release by uploading the signed APK generated in the previous section (15.1). Google Play supports multiple release tracks, including the production track (for the final release) and alpha and beta tracks for testing purposes. You can also set up staged rollouts to gradually release your app to a broader audience.

6. Store Listing Review

Google Play will review your app's store listing to ensure that it complies with their policies. This review includes checking for misleading information, inappropriate content, and adherence to design and branding guidelines. It may take a few hours to several days for the review to complete.

7. App Content Review

In addition to the store listing review, Google Play may conduct a separate review of your app's content. This review checks for any policy violations within the app itself, such as content that violates intellectual property rights or promotes harmful behavior.

8. Publishing

Once your app listing and content have been approved, you can publish your app on the Google Play Store. Users will now be able to discover, download, and install your app on their Android devices.

9. Updates and Maintenance

After the initial release, you'll likely need to provide updates to your app. You can do this by uploading a new version of your APK in the Developer Console. Be sure to communicate any significant changes or improvements to your users through release notes.

10. User Reviews and Ratings

Pay attention to user reviews and ratings on the Play Store. Respond to user feedback, address issues, and engage with your audience. Positive reviews and high ratings can boost your app's visibility and credibility.

11. App Promotion

Promote your app through various channels, including social media, email marketing, and online advertising. Encourage users to rate and review your app. Consider using Google Play's promotional features, such as running advertisements on the platform.

12. Monitor Performance

Regularly monitor your app's performance using analytics tools. Track user engagement, retention rates, and app crashes. This data can help you make informed decisions about updates and improvements.

Remember that the process of submitting an app to the Google Play Store is an ongoing effort. Maintaining and improving your app, engaging with your user community, and staying updated with Android platform changes are all essential aspects of successful app development and distribution.

Section 15.3: App Signing and Distribution

App signing is a crucial step in the Android app distribution process. When you build an Android app, you sign it with a digital certificate to ensure its integrity and authenticity. This section will cover the basics of app signing, including the use of the Android Keystore, and guide you through the distribution process.

1. Android Keystore

The Android Keystore is a secure storage system for cryptographic keys, certificates, and other security-related data. It is used to generate and manage the key pairs required for signing your Android app. The Android Keystore provides a secure and tamper-resistant environment for storing these keys.

To generate a signing key using the Android Keystore, you can use the `keytool` command-line utility or Android Studio's integrated key generation tool. Here's an example of how to generate a signing key using `keytool`:

```
keytool -genkeypair -v -keystore my-release-key.keystore -keyalg RSA -keysize
2048 -validity 10000 -alias my-key-alias
```

This command generates a new keystore file (`my-release-key.keystore`) and a key pair with the alias `my-key-alias`. Make sure to store the keystore file and its password securely, as you'll need it during the app signing process.

2. Signing Your App

Once you have a keystore and key pair, you can sign your Android app's APK with the private key. In Android Studio, you can configure the signing process by going to "Build" > "Build Bundle(s) / APK(s)" > "Build APK(s)" and selecting the keystore file and alias.

Here's a simplified example of how to sign your app using Gradle in your app's `build.gradle` file:

```
android {
    // ...
    signingConfigs {
        release {
            storeFile file('my-release-key.keystore')
            storePassword 'your_keystore_password'
            keyAlias 'my-key-alias'
            keyPassword 'your_key_password'
        }
    }
    buildTypes {
        release {
            signingConfig signingConfigs.release
            // ...
        }
    }
    // ...
}
```

Remember not to store your keystore passwords in version control or expose them in any way. Use secure methods to manage these sensitive credentials.

3. Distributing Your App

Once your app is signed, you can distribute it to users. The most common way to do this is by uploading your app's signed APK to the Google Play Developer Console, as explained in the previous section (15.2). Google Play's distribution platform takes care of delivering updates to users and ensures that your app is securely distributed.

4. App Updates and Versioning

When you release updates to your app, it's important to increase the version code and version name in your app's `build.gradle` file. The version code is an integer value that must be higher for each new release, while the version name is a user-friendly string that can be used to indicate the release's name or version.

```
android {
    // ...
    defaultConfig {
        versionCode 2 // Increment for each release
        versionName "1.1" // Increment for each release
        // ...
    }
    // ...
}
```

By incrementing the version code, you ensure that users receive and install the latest version of your app.

5. App Signing and Security

App signing is critical for security. It allows users to verify that an app hasn't been tampered with since its original release. Android's Package Manager uses the app's digital signature to confirm its authenticity.

In addition to app signing, consider implementing other security measures, such as code obfuscation and runtime permissions, to protect your app and its users from security threats.

By following these app signing and distribution best practices, you can ensure that your Android app is securely signed and distributed to users, providing a reliable and trustworthy experience.

Section 15.4: User Reviews and Ratings

User reviews and ratings are essential aspects of the app publishing process on the Google Play Store. They provide valuable feedback to developers and influence potential users' decisions. In this section, we will explore the importance of user reviews and ratings and how to manage them effectively.

1. The Significance of User Reviews

User reviews serve several purposes:

- **Feedback:** Reviews are a direct channel for users to provide feedback on your app's performance, usability, and features.

- **App Improvement:** Developers can use user reviews to identify bugs, usability issues, or desired features that need improvement or implementation.

- **App Promotion:** Positive reviews and high ratings can boost your app's visibility and credibility on the Google Play Store.

- **User Engagement:** Responding to user reviews demonstrates your commitment to user satisfaction and can lead to increased user engagement.

2. Encouraging User Reviews

To collect user reviews, consider implementing these strategies:

- **In-App Prompts:** Prompt users to leave a review after they've had a positive experience or completed a significant action within the app. Be cautious not to interrupt the user experience.

- **Timed Requests:** Ask for reviews at an appropriate time, such as after a user has successfully completed a task or reached a milestone in your app.

- **Incentives:** Offer rewards or incentives, such as in-app currency or premium features, to users who leave reviews.

- **Polite and Contextual Requests:** Use polite and context-aware messages when requesting reviews. Explain why user feedback is valuable and how it helps improve the app.

3. Responding to User Reviews

Engaging with user reviews is equally important. Here are some guidelines for responding to reviews:

- **Timely Responses:** Respond promptly to both positive and negative reviews. This shows that you value user feedback.

- **Professionalism:** Maintain a professional and respectful tone in your responses, even when addressing critical reviews.

- **Problem Resolution:** For negative reviews, offer solutions or explanations for issues raised. Show users that you are actively working to address their concerns.

- **Acknowledgment:** Acknowledge positive reviews with gratitude and appreciation.

- **Privacy:** Ensure that your responses do not violate user privacy or disclose sensitive information.

Negative reviews are inevitable, but they can be turned into opportunities for improvement:

- **Listen Actively:** Read negative reviews carefully to understand the specific issues users are facing.

- **Respond Thoughtfully:** Address the user's concerns empathetically and offer potential solutions.

- **Update and Improve:** Use negative feedback to identify areas for improvement in your app. Regularly update your app to address these concerns.

Use tools and analytics to track user reviews and ratings over time. This data can help you identify trends, assess the impact of updates, and measure user sentiment. Google Play's Developer Console provides analytics and insights into user reviews and ratings.

Ratings significantly affect an app's visibility on the Play Store. Higher-rated apps tend to rank higher in search results and receive more downloads. Consistently positive reviews and high ratings improve your app's chances of being featured by Google.

In conclusion, user reviews and ratings are vital for the success of your app on the Google Play Store. Encourage users to provide feedback, respond to reviews professionally, and use negative feedback as an opportunity for improvement. By actively managing user reviews, you can enhance your app's reputation, user engagement, and overall success in the Android ecosystem.

Section 15.5: App Updates and Maintenance

App updates and ongoing maintenance are crucial aspects of maintaining a successful Android app. In this section, we'll explore why updates and maintenance are essential and provide best practices for managing them effectively.

1. The Importance of App Updates

App updates serve multiple purposes, including:

- **Bug Fixes:** Addressing bugs and issues that users report or that you discover during testing or monitoring.

- **Security:** Patching vulnerabilities and ensuring that your app remains secure against emerging threats.

- **Performance:** Optimizing the app's performance by identifying and resolving bottlenecks and inefficiencies.

- **Feature Enhancements:** Adding new features or improving existing ones based on user feedback and evolving market trends.

- **Compatibility:** Ensuring that the app remains compatible with the latest Android versions and devices.

- **User Engagement:** Keeping users engaged by offering new content, features, or improvements.

2. Planning App Updates

To effectively plan app updates, consider the following:

- **User Feedback:** Use user reviews, feedback, and analytics to identify areas that need improvement or features that users desire.

- **Release Cycles:** Establish a release schedule that balances the need for regular updates with thorough testing and quality assurance.

- **Versioning:** Follow a clear version numbering scheme to indicate the significance of updates (e.g., major, minor, or patch releases).

- **Changelogs:** Maintain clear changelogs that detail what's new, fixed, or improved in each update. This helps users understand the value of the update.

3. Bug Tracking and Issue Management

Implement a robust bug tracking and issue management system to streamline the process of identifying, prioritizing, and resolving issues. Tools like JIRA, Trello, or GitHub Issues can help you manage this effectively.

4. Security Updates

Security should be a top priority in app maintenance. Regularly review and update libraries, dependencies, and code to address security vulnerabilities. Stay informed about security threats relevant to your app's technology stack and address them promptly.

5. Regression Testing

When making updates, conduct thorough regression testing to ensure that new changes do not introduce new bugs or break existing functionality. Automated testing tools can help streamline this process.

6. User Communication

Communicate with your users about updates:

- **Announcements:** Use release notes, in-app notifications, or email to inform users about significant updates and new features.

- **Feedback Channels:** Encourage users to provide feedback on new updates, and be responsive to their comments.

7. App Store Guidelines

Ensure that your updates comply with app store guidelines. Updates that violate these guidelines can result in your app's removal from the store.

8. Backward Compatibility

While adding new features, maintain backward compatibility with previous app versions whenever possible. This ensures that users with older app versions can still use your service.

9. Performance Monitoring

Regularly monitor your app's performance. Use crash reporting tools to identify and fix issues that cause crashes or slowdowns.

10. User Data and Privacy

Handle user data with care and in compliance with privacy regulations. Be transparent about data usage in your app and seek user consent when necessary.

11. User Support

Provide user support channels, such as help centers or customer support email, to assist users who encounter issues or have questions about the app.

12. Continuous Improvement

App maintenance is an ongoing process. Continuously gather user feedback, analyze app performance, and make data-driven decisions to improve the user experience.

In conclusion, app updates and maintenance are essential for keeping your Android app relevant, secure, and well-received by users. By planning updates, addressing bugs, enhancing security, and maintaining clear communication with users, you can ensure the long-term success and quality of your Android application.

Chapter 16: Kotlin Coroutines

Section 16.1: Introduction to Kotlin Coroutines

Kotlin Coroutines are a powerful and flexible way to write asynchronous, non-blocking code in a more structured and readable manner. They simplify the management of concurrency and allow you to write asynchronous code that looks like regular synchronous code, making it easier to understand and maintain. In this section, we'll provide an introduction to Kotlin Coroutines and their key concepts.

1. What Are Kotlin Coroutines?

Kotlin Coroutines are a feature of the Kotlin programming language that allows you to write asynchronous code sequentially. They are essentially lightweight threads that can be used to perform tasks concurrently without the overhead of creating and managing traditional threads.

2. Why Use Coroutines?

There are several reasons to use Kotlin Coroutines in your Android applications:

- **Simplicity:** Coroutines provide a high-level and structured way to write asynchronous code, making it easier to reason about and debug.

- **Concurrent Operations:** You can run multiple asynchronous tasks concurrently without managing threads manually.

- **Cancellation:** Coroutines support cancellation, allowing you to cancel ongoing tasks when they are no longer needed.

- **Suspend Functions:** Coroutines work well with suspend functions, which can be used to perform asynchronous operations in a sequential, non-blocking manner.

3. Key Concepts

3.1. CoroutineScope

A CoroutineScope defines the context in which a coroutine runs. It provides a structured way to start and manage coroutines. In Android, you often create a CoroutineScope associated with a lifecycle component like an Activity or Fragment.

3.2. launch and async

Two common ways to start coroutines are launch and async.

- launch: Use it when you want to start a coroutine that performs a task concurrently without returning a result.

- **async:** Use it when you want to start a coroutine that performs a task concurrently and returns a result.

3.3. suspend Functions

Suspend functions are a key component of coroutines. They can be paused and resumed, allowing you to write asynchronous code that looks like sequential code. Functions that perform I/O or other blocking operations should be marked as `suspend`.

3.4. Dispatcher

A `Dispatcher` defines the thread or thread pool on which a coroutine runs. Common dispatchers include `Dispatchers.Main` for the main/UI thread and `Dispatchers.IO` for I/O-bound tasks.

4. Getting Started

To use Kotlin Coroutines in your Android project, you need to add the `kotlinx-coroutines-android` library to your dependencies. Then, you can create a `CoroutineScope`, launch coroutines, and use `suspend` functions to perform asynchronous tasks.

```
implementation "org.jetbrains.kotlinx:kotlinx-coroutines-android:1.5.2"
```

```kotlin
import kotlinx.coroutines.CoroutineScope
import kotlinx.coroutines.Dispatchers
import kotlinx.coroutines.launch

val coroutineScope = CoroutineScope(Dispatchers.Main)

coroutineScope.launch {
    // Your asynchronous code here
}
```

5. Benefits of Kotlin Coroutines

Kotlin Coroutines offer several advantages for Android development:

- **Readability:** Coroutines make asynchronous code more readable and maintainable.

- **Performance:** They are lightweight and efficient, reducing the overhead of thread management.

- **Cancellation:** Coroutines provide built-in support for canceling tasks.

- **Testing:** Coroutines can be easily tested using testing frameworks like `runBlockingTest`.

In the next sections, we will explore various use cases and advanced topics related to Kotlin Coroutines in Android development.

Section 16.2: Asynchronous Programming with Coroutines

In the previous section, we introduced Kotlin Coroutines and their key concepts. Now, let's dive deeper into how coroutines enable asynchronous programming in Android. Asynchronous programming is crucial for handling tasks that may take some time to complete, such as network requests, database operations, and file I/O.

1. Suspending Functions

Suspending functions are a fundamental component of coroutines. They are functions that can be paused and resumed. You mark a function as `suspend` when it performs an operation that may block, such as making a network request. This allows you to write asynchronous code that looks sequential.

Here's an example of a simple `suspend` function:

```kotlin
suspend fun fetchUserData(userId: String): User {
    // Simulate a network request delay
    delay(1000)

    // Perform the network request and return the user data
    return apiService.getUser(userId)
}
```

In this example, the `delay` function simulates a network request delay, and the `getUser` function is a suspend function that fetches user data.

2. Launching Coroutines

To execute a suspending function asynchronously, you can use the `launch` coroutine builder. It starts a new coroutine and doesn't return a result. For example:

```kotlin
coroutineScope.launch {
    val user = fetchUserData("123")
    // Update the UI with user data
    updateUI(user)
}
```

In this code, `fetchUserData` is called from within a coroutine, allowing it to run concurrently without blocking the main thread. Once the user data is fetched, you can update the UI accordingly.

3. Async-Await Pattern

Sometimes, you need to execute multiple asynchronous tasks concurrently and wait for their results. This is where the `async` coroutine builder comes in handy. It allows you to start a coroutine that computes a result asynchronously and returns a `Deferred` object, which is a promise for the result.

Here's an example of using `async` to fetch two user profiles concurrently and await their results:

```
val deferredUser1 = coroutineScope.async { fetchUserData("123") }
val deferredUser2 = coroutineScope.async { fetchUserData("456") }

val user1 = deferredUser1.await()
val user2 = deferredUser2.await()

// Process user1 and user2
```

In this example, we start two coroutines to fetch user data concurrently, and then we await their results. This pattern is useful for parallelizing tasks.

4. Exception Handling

Coroutines provide structured exception handling. You can use `try-catch` blocks within coroutines to handle exceptions gracefully. For example:

```
coroutineScope.launch {
    try {
        val result = riskyOperation()
        // Handle the result
    } catch (e: Exception) {
        // Handle the exception
    }
}
```

5. Coroutine Context

Coroutines run in a context defined by a `CoroutineScope`. You can specify a dispatcher that determines which thread the coroutine runs on. Common dispatchers include `Dispatchers.Main` for the main/UI thread and `Dispatchers.IO` for I/O-bound tasks. It's essential to choose the right dispatcher based on the task to ensure the app's responsiveness.

In this section, we explored how suspending functions, coroutine builders, and exception handling work in Kotlin Coroutines for asynchronous programming in Android. In the next section, we'll delve into handling concurrency and managing multiple coroutines effectively.

Section 16.3: Handling Concurrency

Concurrency is a critical aspect of modern Android app development. In this section, we will explore how Kotlin Coroutines can help you manage concurrency effectively.

1. Concurrent Operations

With Coroutines, you can easily execute multiple operations concurrently. Consider a scenario where you want to download two images from the internet simultaneously. You can use the `async` coroutine builder to achieve this:

```
val deferredImage1 = async(Dispatchers.IO) { downloadImage("url1") }
val deferredImage2 = async(Dispatchers.IO) { downloadImage("url2") }

val image1 = deferredImage1.await()
val image2 = deferredImage2.await()

// Process the downloaded images
```

In this code, `downloadImage` is a suspend function that downloads an image from a given URL. By using `async` with the `await` function, you can initiate both downloads concurrently and wait for their results.

2. Concurrent Dispatchers

Coroutines allow you to specify different dispatchers for concurrent tasks. For instance, you might want to perform CPU-intensive tasks on a background thread and UI-related tasks on the main thread. You can achieve this using the `withContext` function:

```
coroutineScope.launch(Dispatchers.Main) {
    val result = withContext(Dispatchers.IO) {
        // Perform a CPU-intensive task
        computeSomeResult()
    }
    // Update the UI with the result
    updateUI(result)
}
```

In this example, we launch a coroutine on the main dispatcher, but we switch to the IO dispatcher using `withContext` for the CPU-intensive computation. Afterward, we return to the main dispatcher to update the UI.

3. CoroutineScope

Managing the lifecycles of concurrent coroutines is crucial to prevent memory leaks. You can use a `CoroutineScope` to handle this. For example, in an Android `ViewModel`, you can create a `CoroutineScope` tied to the ViewModel's lifecycle:

```
class MyViewModel : ViewModel() {
    private val viewModelScope = CoroutineScope(Dispatchers.Main)

    fun performTasks() {
        viewModelScope.launch {
            // Perform concurrent tasks
        }
```

```
    }

    override fun onCleared() {
        super.onCleared()
        viewModelScope.cancel() // Cancel all coroutines when ViewModel is cl
eared
    }
}
```

By canceling the CoroutineScope when it's no longer needed, you ensure that any ongoing coroutines are canceled, preventing memory leaks.

4. Thread-Safe Data Access

Kotlin Coroutines offer built-in mechanisms to ensure thread-safe data access. The Mutex class allows you to protect shared resources from concurrent access:

```
val mutex = Mutex()
var sharedData: Int = 0

coroutineScope.launch(Dispatchers.IO) {
    mutex.withLock {
        // Access and modify sharedData safely
        sharedData++
    }
}
```

By using withLock, you guarantee that only one coroutine can access the shared data at a time, preventing data corruption.

5. Parallel Map and Filter

Kotlin Coroutines simplify parallel operations on collections using the map and filter functions. For instance, to apply a function to a list of items concurrently:

```
val items = listOf(1, 2, 3, 4, 5)
val results = items.map { item ->
    async(Dispatchers.IO) {
        processItem(item)
    }
}.awaitAll()
```

In this code, processItem is applied to each item in parallel, and awaitAll collects the results.

In this section, we explored how Kotlin Coroutines can be used to handle concurrency effectively in Android apps. Whether you need to execute concurrent tasks, manage different dispatchers, or ensure thread-safe data access, Kotlin Coroutines provide the tools to simplify these complex operations. In the next section, we'll explore the use of the Flow API for reactive programming with coroutines.

Section 16.4: Flow API for Reactive Programming

Reactive programming is a popular paradigm for handling asynchronous data streams in Android apps. Kotlin Coroutines provide the Flow API, which is a powerful tool for reactive programming.

1. Introduction to Flow

A Flow is a cold asynchronous data stream that can emit multiple values over time. It is similar to an Observable in RxJava or a Publisher in Reactive Streams. You can create a Flow using the flow builder:

```
val flow = flow {
    emit(1)
    emit(2)
    emit(3)
}
```

In this example, the flow emits the integers 1, 2, and 3 sequentially.

2. Flow Operators

Flow provides a rich set of operators for transforming and processing data streams. For example, you can use the map operator to transform emitted values:

```
val doubledFlow = flow {
    emit(1)
    emit(2)
    emit(3)
}.map { it * 2 }
```

Now, doubledFlow will emit 2, 4, and 6.

3. Collecting a Flow

To consume the values emitted by a Flow, you use the collect function. It suspends the coroutine until the Flow completes:

```
doubledFlow.collect { value ->
    println(value)
}
```

This code will print:

```
2
4
6
```

4. Flow on Dispatchers

You can specify the dispatcher on which the `Flow` should be executed. For example, to perform a network request on the IO dispatcher and collect the result on the main dispatcher:

```
flow {
    val result = networkRequest() // Perform a suspend function for network r
equest
    emit(result)
}.flowOn(Dispatchers.IO)
 .collect { result ->
    // Update UI on the main thread
    updateUI(result)
}
```

By using `flowOn`, you ensure that the network request runs on a background thread, preventing UI blocking.

5. Cancellation of Flows

`Flow` integrates seamlessly with coroutine cancellation. When the collecting coroutine is canceled, the flow's execution is also canceled:

```
val job = CoroutineScope(Dispatchers.Main).launch {
    flow {
        repeat(1000) { i ->
            delay(100)
            emit(i)
        }
    }.collect { value ->
        println(value)
    }
    delay(250) // After 250ms, cancel the job
    job.cancel()
}
```

In this example, the flow will be canceled after 250ms, and the coroutine will stop emitting values.

6. Error Handling

`Flow` supports error handling through the `catch` operator. You can handle exceptions emitted by the flow:

```
flow {
    emit(1)
    throw Exception("An error occurred")
}.catch { e ->
    println("Flow exception: $e")
}.collect { value ->
```

```
    println(value)
}
```

The catch operator allows you to handle errors gracefully without affecting the flow's execution.

Kotlin Flow is a powerful tool for implementing reactive programming in Android apps. Whether you're dealing with asynchronous data streams, transforming data, or handling errors, Flow provides a concise and expressive way to work with asynchronous data. In the next section, we'll explore some common use cases and practical examples of Kotlin Coroutines in Android development.

Section 16.5: Coroutine Use Cases in Android

In this section, we'll explore various practical use cases of Kotlin Coroutines in Android app development. Kotlin Coroutines simplify asynchronous programming, making it easier to handle background tasks, network requests, and concurrency. Let's dive into some common scenarios where Coroutines shine.

1. Asynchronous Network Requests

One of the most common use cases for Coroutines is performing asynchronous network requests. You can use the async builder to execute network requests concurrently and await their results:

```
val result1 = async { fetchDataFromServer1() }
val result2 = async { fetchDataFromServer2() }

val combinedResult = result1.await() + result2.await()
```

Here, we initiate two network requests concurrently and combine their results when both are complete.

2. Sequential Background Tasks

Coroutines make it easy to perform a series of background tasks sequentially. For example, you might need to fetch data from a database, perform some computation, and then update the UI. You can use async and await for this:

```
val data = async(Dispatchers.IO) { fetchDataFromDatabase() }
val processedData = async(Dispatchers.Default) { processData(data.await()) }
withContext(Dispatchers.Main) {
    updateUI(processedData)
}
```

This code ensures that each step runs on the appropriate dispatcher while keeping the code structured and readable.

3. Debouncing Search Queries

When implementing a search feature, you can use Coroutines to debounce user input, preventing excessive network requests. By adding a delay before executing the search, you can reduce the load on the server:

```
private var searchJob: Job? = null

fun onSearchQueryChanged(query: String) {
    searchJob?.cancel()
    searchJob = CoroutineScope(Dispatchers.Main).launch {
        delay(300) // Debounce by waiting for 300ms of inactivity
        val result = search(query)
        updateUI(result)
    }
}
```

This code cancels any ongoing search job when a new query is entered and only triggers a search if there's a 300ms gap in user input.

4. UI Background Threads

Coroutines simplify switching between UI and background threads. You can use the withContext function to safely update the UI from a background thread:

```
CoroutineScope(Dispatchers.IO).launch {
    val result = fetchDataFromServer()
    withContext(Dispatchers.Main) {
        updateUI(result)
    }
}
```

This pattern ensures that UI updates occur on the main thread, preventing crashes and UI inconsistencies.

5. Handling Errors Gracefully

Kotlin Coroutines provide exceptional error-handling capabilities. You can use try-catch blocks within Coroutines to handle exceptions gracefully:

```
try {
    val result = async { fetchRemoteData() }.await()
    // Process the result
} catch (e: Exception) {
    // Handle the error
    showErrorDialog(e.message ?: "An error occurred")
}
```

By wrapping asynchronous code in a try-catch block, you can catch and handle exceptions without crashing the app.

6. Complex Workflows

In Android development, you often encounter complex workflows involving multiple asynchronous operations. Coroutines allow you to structure these workflows sequentially while keeping the code readable:

```
val result1 = fetchDataFromServer()
val result2 = processData(result1)
val result3 = saveDataToDatabase(result2)
updateUI(result3)
```

This straightforward approach enhances code maintainability and reduces callback hell.

Kotlin Coroutines have become an essential tool for Android developers, simplifying asynchronous programming and making code more readable and maintainable. Whether you're handling network requests, database operations, or complex workflows, Coroutines can help you write clean and efficient Android apps. In the next chapter, we'll explore advanced Android topics, including customization, native development, augmented reality, and machine learning, to take your Android development skills to the next level.

Chapter 17: Advanced Android Topics

Section 17.1: Customizing Android ROMs and System UI

In this section, we'll delve into the advanced topic of customizing Android ROMs (Read-Only Memory) and the system user interface (UI). While most Android app development occurs within the boundaries of official Android releases, there's a dedicated community of developers and enthusiasts who create custom ROMs and tweak the system UI to offer unique user experiences. This section provides an overview of this fascinating world of Android customization.

Custom ROMs

A custom ROM is a modified version of the Android operating system that can be installed on Android devices. These ROMs are created by developers, often as a hobby or passion project. Custom ROMs can provide various benefits:

1. **Enhanced Performance**: Custom ROMs are often optimized for better performance, which can lead to improved device speed and responsiveness.

2. **Additional Features**: Developers can add features not present in the stock Android version, such as additional customization options, improved privacy settings, and unique user interfaces.

3. **Regular Updates**: Some custom ROMs receive updates more frequently than official Android releases, ensuring that users have access to the latest security patches and features.

4. **Debloating**: Custom ROMs may come without the bloatware (pre-installed apps) that carriers and manufacturers often include on Android devices.

5. **Extended Device Lifespan**: Older devices that no longer receive official updates can benefit from custom ROMs, which can extend the device's usable lifespan.

Rooting

To install a custom ROM, you typically need to root your Android device. Rooting gives you superuser or administrative access, allowing you to modify the system files and settings that are usually off-limits. It's essential to note that rooting can void your device's warranty and potentially introduce security risks. Therefore, it should be done with caution and an understanding of the potential consequences.

Customization of System UI

Beyond custom ROMs, Android enthusiasts often customize the system UI to personalize their devices further. Some common ways to customize the system UI include:

1. **Custom Launchers**: Android launchers replace the default home screen and app drawer, allowing users to change the look and behavior of their device's interface.

2. **Icon Packs**: Users can install icon packs to change the appearance of app icons throughout the system.

3. **Widgets**: Widgets provide at-a-glance information and quick access to app features. Users can choose from various widget options and sizes.

4. **Themes**: Some Android versions and devices support theming, enabling users to change the overall color scheme, fonts, and icons.

5. **System Animations**: Enthusiasts can adjust system animations, such as transitions between app screens and the speed of UI elements.

While customization can provide a unique Android experience, it's essential to be aware of potential downsides, such as reduced system stability, security risks, and compatibility issues with official updates. Furthermore, not all Android devices support extensive customization, so the degree to which you can personalize your device may vary.

In this section, we've introduced the concept of custom ROMs and system UI customization, providing an overview of the possibilities and considerations when venturing into the world of advanced Android customization. In the subsequent sections, we'll explore other advanced Android topics, including native development, augmented reality, machine learning, and building apps for foldable and dual-screen devices.

Section 17.2: Android NDK and Native Development

In this section, we'll dive into Android NDK (Native Development Kit), a set of tools that allows you to develop Android apps using native code languages like C and C++. While most Android app development is done using Java or Kotlin, there are scenarios where using native code can be beneficial.

Why Use Native Development?

1. **Performance Optimization**: Native code can be more efficient than Java or Kotlin for certain tasks, especially those that involve complex calculations or heavy processing. Games and multimedia applications often benefit from native development.

2. **Legacy Code**: If you have existing C or C++ libraries that you want to reuse in your Android app, the NDK provides a way to integrate them seamlessly.

3. **Low-Level Access**: Native development allows you to access hardware-specific features and interact with low-level system components.

4. **Cross-Platform Development**: If you're developing a cross-platform app that needs to run on both Android and iOS, sharing a common C or C++ codebase can be advantageous.

Setting Up the Android NDK

To start using the Android NDK, you need to set it up in your development environment. Follow these steps:

1. **Install Android NDK**: Download and install the Android NDK from the official Android Developers website.

2. **Configure Your Project**: In your Android Studio project, create a new module for native code. This module will contain your native C/C++ code files.

3. **Write Native Code**: Write your C/C++ code in the native module. You can use Android Studio's CMake or ndk-build to build your native code.

4. **Integrate Native Code**: To use native code in your Java or Kotlin code, you'll need to create a JNI (Java Native Interface) bridge. This allows your Java/Kotlin code to call functions from your native code.

Example: Using Native Code for Performance

Let's consider an example where native development can significantly boost performance. Suppose you're developing an image processing application that needs to apply complex filters to high-resolution images. Implementing this in Java/Kotlin might be slow due to the interpreted nature of these languages.

```cpp
#include <jni.h>
#include <opencv2/opencv.hpp>

extern "C" JNIEXPORT void JNICALL
Java_com_example_imageprocessing_ImageProcessor_applyFilter(
        JNIEnv *env,
        jobject instance,
        jlong inputMatAddr,
        jlong outputMatAddr) {
    cv::Mat &inputMat = *(cv::Mat *) inputMatAddr;
    cv::Mat &outputMat = *(cv::Mat *) outputMatAddr;

    // Apply a custom image filter using OpenCV
    cv::Mat kernel = (cv::Mat_<char>(3, 3) << 0, -1, 0, -1, 5, -1, 0, -1, 0);
    cv::filter2D(inputMat, outputMat, -1, kernel);
}
```

In this example, we've used OpenCV, a popular open-source computer vision library, to apply a custom image filter in native C++ code. The JNI bridge allows this native code to be called from Java/Kotlin.

Considerations

While native development can offer performance benefits, it also comes with challenges:

1. **Complexity**: Native code is generally more complex and error-prone than Java/Kotlin, so it's crucial to have strong debugging and testing practices.

2. **Portability**: Native code is platform-specific, so you might need to maintain different versions for different architectures (e.g., ARM and x86).

3. **Security**: Incorrectly written native code can introduce security vulnerabilities, so careful coding and code reviews are essential.

In this section, we've explored the Android NDK and native development, highlighting its advantages, setup process, and providing an example of how it can be used to improve performance in Android applications. Native development is a valuable tool in an Android developer's toolkit, but it should be used judiciously based on specific project requirements.

Section 17.3: Augmented Reality with ARCore

Augmented Reality (AR) is a technology that overlays digital content onto the real world, enhancing the user's perception of reality. Google's ARCore is a platform that enables developers to create AR experiences for Android devices. In this section, we'll delve into ARCore and explore how to develop augmented reality applications.

What is ARCore?

ARCore is Google's software development kit (SDK) for building AR applications on Android devices. It provides a set of tools and APIs that allow developers to create interactive, location-based, and immersive AR experiences. ARCore works with a wide range of Android devices, making it accessible to a broad user base.

Key Features of ARCore

1. **Motion Tracking**: ARCore can track the device's position and orientation, enabling stable and accurate placement of virtual objects in the real world.

2. **Environmental Understanding**: It can detect flat surfaces like floors, tables, and walls, allowing you to position AR objects realistically.

3. **Light Estimation**: ARCore can estimate the ambient lighting conditions, allowing virtual objects to blend seamlessly with the real environment.

4. **Cloud Anchors**: With Cloud Anchors, you can create shared AR experiences where multiple users see and interact with the same virtual objects in real-time.

To get started with ARCore development, follow these steps:

1. **Install ARCore**: Ensure that the user's device has ARCore installed. You can prompt users to install it if necessary.

2. **Set Up the Development Environment**: Use Android Studio and the ARCore SDK to create an AR project.

3. **Add AR Objects**: Develop 3D models or animations for your AR experience and add them to your project.

4. **Implement AR Functionality**: Write code to interact with ARCore, including motion tracking, surface detection, and object placement.

5. **Testing**: Test your AR app on ARCore-compatible devices to ensure that virtual objects behave as expected in the real world.

Here's a simple example of how to add a virtual object to the AR scene using ARCore:

```java
// Initialize ARCore session
ArSession arSession = new ArSession(this);

// Create an AR scene view
ArSceneView arSceneView = new ArSceneView(this);
arSceneView.setupSession(arSession);

// Create a 3D model
ModelRenderable modelRenderable = ModelRenderable.builder()
        .setSource(this, R.raw.my_3d_model)
        .build();

// Create an anchor at a specific location
Anchor anchor = arSession.createAnchor(new Pose(new float[]{0, 0, -2}, new fl
oat[]{0, 0, 0, 1}));

// Attach the model to the anchor
AnchorNode anchorNode = new AnchorNode(anchor);
anchorNode.setRenderable(modelRenderable);

// Add the anchor node to the AR scene
arSceneView.getScene().addChild(anchorNode);
```

This code initializes an AR session, loads a 3D model, creates an anchor in the AR world, and attaches the model to that anchor.

Use Cases for ARCore

ARCore can be used for various applications, including:

- **Gaming**: Create interactive and immersive mobile games with AR elements.
- **Education**: Develop educational apps that bring subjects to life through AR.
- **Navigation**: Enhance navigation apps with AR directions and real-world information overlays.
- **Retail**: Allow customers to visualize products in their real environment before purchasing.
- **Interior Design**: Assist users in visualizing furniture and decor in their homes.

ARCore offers endless possibilities for creating engaging and interactive experiences on Android devices, making it an exciting technology for developers to explore and leverage.

In this section, we've introduced ARCore and explored its key features, development process, and a simple example of adding a virtual object to an AR scene. Augmented reality opens up new dimensions for Android app development, enabling innovative and immersive user experiences.

Section 17.4: Machine Learning with Android

Machine learning (ML) is a rapidly advancing field that empowers Android developers to create intelligent and data-driven applications. In this section, we'll explore the integration of machine learning into Android apps and discuss the tools and libraries available to make this possible.

Machine Learning on Android

Bringing machine learning models to Android devices allows applications to make predictions, classify data, and understand user behavior. This opens up opportunities for creating personalized experiences, enhancing image and voice recognition, and automating decision-making processes.

TensorFlow and TensorFlow Lite

TensorFlow is an open-source machine learning framework developed by Google. TensorFlow Lite is a lightweight version of TensorFlow designed for mobile and embedded devices, making it ideal for Android app integration. TensorFlow Lite allows you to run machine learning models efficiently on Android smartphones and tablets.

To integrate TensorFlow Lite into your Android project, follow these steps:

1. **Add TensorFlow Lite Dependency**: Include the TensorFlow Lite library in your project's dependencies.

2. **Model Conversion**: Convert your trained machine learning model to TensorFlow Lite format using tools like `tflite_convert`.

3. **Model Integration**: Load the TensorFlow Lite model into your Android app using the TensorFlow Lite interpreter.

4. **Inference**: Use the interpreter to make inferences or predictions based on the model's input.

Here's a simplified example of loading and running a TensorFlow Lite model in an Android app:

```
// Load the TensorFlow Lite model
Interpreter interpreter = new Interpreter(loadModelFile("my_model.tflite"));

// Prepare input data
float[][] input = preprocessInputData(image);

// Run inference
float[][] output = new float[1][numClasses];
interpreter.run(input, output);

// Process the output
int predictedClass = postprocessOutput(output);
```

This code loads a TensorFlow Lite model, prepares input data (e.g., an image), runs inference, and processes the output to make predictions.

1. **Image Classification**: Identify objects or scenes within images.

2. **Object Detection**: Locate and recognize specific objects within images or camera feeds.

3. **Natural Language Processing (NLP)**: Analyze and understand text data, including sentiment analysis and language translation.

4. **Voice Recognition**: Enable voice commands and speech-to-text capabilities.

5. **Recommendation Systems**: Provide personalized content or product recommendations.

6. **Anomaly Detection**: Identify unusual patterns or outliers in data.

7. **Gesture Recognition**: Recognize gestures made by users.

ML Libraries and Tools

In addition to TensorFlow and TensorFlow Lite, there are several ML libraries and tools available for Android development:

- **ML Kit for Firebase**: A Google-powered mobile SDK that provides ready-to-use machine learning features, including text recognition, image labeling, and face detection.

- **scikit-learn**: A Python library for machine learning that can be integrated into Android apps using tools like Chaquopy or Pyjnius.

- **ONNX Runtime**: An open-source inference engine that supports ONNX (Open Neural Network Exchange) models, which can be used in Android.

- **Custom Models**: You can train your custom machine learning models using popular frameworks like PyTorch or scikit-learn and then convert them to TensorFlow Lite for Android deployment.

Integrating machine learning into Android applications offers endless possibilities for creating intelligent and responsive apps. It's crucial to choose the right tools, models, and libraries based on your application's requirements and constraints. As the field of machine learning continues to evolve, Android developers have access to increasingly powerful and accessible ML capabilities to enhance their apps.

Section 17.5: Building for Foldable and Dual-Screen Devices

Foldable and dual-screen devices are an exciting evolution in the Android ecosystem, offering new possibilities for app design and user experiences. In this section, we'll explore the concepts of building apps for foldable and dual-screen Android devices and how to make the most of their unique form factors.

Understanding Foldable and Dual-Screen Devices

Foldable devices have screens that can be folded or unfolded, allowing users to switch between phone and tablet modes. Dual-screen devices, on the other hand, consist of two separate screens connected by a hinge, enabling a variety of multitasking scenarios.

Key Terminology:
- **Main Screen**: The primary screen that is visible when the device is in its default folded state.

- **Cover Screen**: The smaller screen on the outside of the device, visible when folded.

- **Hinge**: The physical mechanism that allows the device to fold and unfold.

Design Considerations

Designing for foldable and dual-screen devices requires a user-centric approach. Consider the following factors:

1. Screen Continuity:

Ensure a seamless transition between screens. Apps should adapt to changes in screen size and orientation without interruption.

2. Multitasking:

Leverage the additional screen real estate for multitasking. Allow users to run multiple app instances, drag and drop content between screens, or display complementary information.

3. App Continuity:

Enable your app to continue seamlessly between screens. Users should be able to start a task on one screen and continue it on the other.

4. Flex Mode:

Take advantage of flex mode on foldable devices, where the device is partially folded, allowing for unique app layouts and experiences.

Android Features for Foldable and Dual-Screen Devices

Android provides several features and APIs to support foldable and dual-screen devices:

1. Screen Hinge Angle:

You can determine the hinge angle programmatically to adapt your app's UI and functionality based on how the device is folded.

2. App Pairing:

Enable app pairs that run side by side on dual-screen devices, enhancing multitasking and collaboration.

3. Resizeable Activities:

Use the Android API to create resizeable activities that automatically adjust to changes in screen size.

4. WindowManager:

Access WindowManager features to manage how your app's windows are displayed across screens.

Code Example: Handling Screen Modes

Here's an example of how to handle screen modes in an Android app for foldable devices:

```
if (isFoldableDevice()) {
    // Check the hinge angle
    float hingeAngle = getHingeAngle();

    if (hingeAngle > 0 && hingeAngle < 180) {
        // Device is partially folded (flex mode)
        adjustLayoutForFlexMode();
    } else if (hingeAngle >= 180) {
        // Device is fully folded, use the cover screen
        switchToCoverScreenLayout();
    } else {
        // Device is unfolded, use the main screen
        switchToMainScreenLayout();
    }
}
```

```
} else {
    // Handle non-foldable devices
    handleRegularLayout();
}
```

This code snippet demonstrates how to adjust your app's layout based on the hinge angle and the state of the foldable device.

Conclusion

Building apps for foldable and dual-screen devices opens up exciting opportunities for innovative user experiences. By considering screen continuity, multitasking, and app continuity, and by utilizing Android's foldable device features, you can create apps that take full advantage of this emerging technology and provide users with a seamless and versatile experience. As these devices become more prevalent, designing for foldables and dual screens will become an essential skill for Android developers.

Chapter 18: Accessibility and Inclusivity

In the modern world, creating inclusive digital experiences is not only a legal requirement in many countries but also a moral obligation. Ensuring that your Android app is accessible to all users, including those with disabilities, is an essential part of responsible app development. In this chapter, we'll delve into accessibility features in Android and learn how to design, test, and promote inclusivity within your applications.

Section 18.1: Accessibility Features in Android

Android provides a wide range of accessibility features and tools to make apps usable by individuals with various disabilities. These features not only enhance the user experience for people with disabilities but also benefit all users in different situations. Let's explore some key accessibility features in Android:

1. *TalkBack*: *TalkBack is Android's built-in screen reader, which provides spoken feedback to users with visual impairments. It reads aloud the content and actions on the screen, allowing users to navigate and interact with the device.*

2. *Accessibility Services*: *Android allows developers to create custom accessibility services that assist users with specific needs. These services can provide alternative navigation methods, input methods, or additional context.*

3. *Text-to-Speech (TTS)*: *Android offers Text-to-Speech capabilities, enabling your app to convert text into spoken words. This can benefit users with visual impairments or those who prefer audio feedback.*

4. *High Contrast Text*: *High Contrast Text mode enhances text legibility by adjusting text and background colors. This can be helpful for users with low vision or color blindness.*

5. *Magnification Gestures*: *Users can magnify parts of the screen with simple gestures, making it easier to read small text or examine details.*

6. *Closed Captions and Subtitles*: *For multimedia content, Android supports closed captions and subtitles, ensuring that users with hearing impairments can access audio content.*

7. *Customizable Display Size and Font*: *Users can adjust the display size and font size to suit their visual preferences, making text and UI elements more readable.*

8. *Voice Access*: *Voice Access allows users to control their device using voice commands, which can be particularly beneficial for users with mobility impairments.*

9. *Gesture Navigation*: *Android's gesture navigation system provides an alternative to traditional button-based navigation, offering users with dexterity issues an easier way to interact with the device.*

10. *Accessibility Scanner*: *The Accessibility Scanner tool analyzes your app for accessibility issues and provides recommendations for improvements.*

Designing for Accessibility

Designing for accessibility involves considering the diverse needs of users from the outset of your app development process. Here are some key principles to keep in mind:

- **Provide Descriptive Content**: Use meaningful and descriptive labels for UI elements, images, and buttons. Ensure that screen readers can convey the purpose of each element.

- **Proper Use of Content Descriptors**: Use content descriptions for images and other non-text elements, so that screen readers can provide context.

- **Keyboard and Touch Navigation**: Ensure that all UI elements are navigable and usable with both touch gestures and keyboard input.

- **Contrast and Color Choices**: Use sufficient contrast between text and background colors to enhance legibility. Avoid relying solely on color to convey information.

- **Resizable Text and Scalable UI**: Design layouts that accommodate resizable text and scalable user interfaces. Avoid fixed layouts that may cause content clipping or text truncation.

- **Testing with Accessibility Services**: Regularly test your app using Android's accessibility services and tools to identify and fix issues.

Conclusion

Accessibility should be a fundamental consideration in every Android app development project. By implementing accessibility features and following best practices in design and testing, you can create apps that are not only legally compliant but also user-friendly for individuals with disabilities. Promoting inclusivity in your apps is not just good practice; it also opens up your app to a wider audience and demonstrates your commitment to making technology accessible to everyone.

Section 18.2: Designing for Accessibility

Designing Android apps with accessibility in mind is crucial to ensure that all users, including those with disabilities, can use your application effectively. Accessibility design goes beyond implementing features; it's about creating a user experience that is inclusive by design. In this section, we'll delve into the principles and best practices for designing Android apps that are accessible to everyone.

Understanding the Importance of Accessibility

Accessibility design is not just a legal requirement; it's an ethical and user-centric approach to app development. By making your app accessible, you ensure that individuals with disabilities can fully engage with your product, opening it up to a wider audience. Moreover, accessibility features often benefit all users in various situations, such as when using the app in noisy environments or with limited dexterity.

Key Principles of Accessibility Design

1. **Perceivable**: Ensure that all information and user interface components are presented in a way that can be perceived by all users. This includes providing text alternatives for non-text content like images, videos, and audio.

2. **Operable**: Design your app so that it can be easily operated by users, regardless of their abilities or the devices they use. This involves making interactive elements, such as buttons and links, easily clickable or tappable.

3. **Understandable**: Create a clear and understandable user interface. Users should be able to comprehend the content and the operation of your app without ambiguity.

4. **Robust**: Develop your app to be robust and compatible with current and future technologies. Avoid using deprecated or non-standard features that might hinder accessibility.

Best Practices for Accessibility Design

1. **Use Semantic Markup**: Ensure that your app's UI elements are semantically marked up with appropriate labels and roles. This helps assistive technologies interpret and convey the content correctly.

2. **Provide Text Alternatives**: Include descriptive text alternatives for images, buttons, and other non-text elements. Screen readers use these descriptions to provide context to users.

3. **Use High Contrast**: Ensure good contrast between text and background colors. This aids users with low vision or color blindness in reading content.

4. **Keyboard Accessibility**: Make sure all interactive elements in your app can be navigated and activated using the keyboard. Implement keyboard shortcuts and focus indicators.

5. **Avoid Solely Color-Reliant Information**: Don't rely solely on color to convey information. Use other cues, such as text labels or icons, to supplement color coding.

6. **Support Scalable Text**: Allow users to resize text without breaking your app's layout. Ensure that the UI remains functional and readable at different text sizes.

7. **Test with Assistive Technologies**: Regularly test your app with screen readers and other assistive technologies to identify and fix issues. Familiarize yourself with the Android Accessibility Scanner tool.

Accessibility in Material Design

Google's Material Design guidelines include specific recommendations for accessibility. When designing your app's user interface, follow these guidelines to create an accessible and visually appealing experience. Material Design encourages the use of legible typography, meaningful color choices, and interactive components that are easy to perceive and operate.

Conclusion

Designing Android apps with accessibility in mind is not just about compliance but also about creating an inclusive and user-friendly experience. By following the principles and best practices outlined in this section, you can ensure that your app is accessible to a broader range of users, including those with disabilities. Accessibility design benefits everyone and is a step toward making technology more inclusive and equitable.

Section 18.3: Testing Accessibility

Ensuring that your Android app is accessible to all users, including those with disabilities, is a critical part of the development process. While designing for accessibility is essential, testing your app for accessibility issues is equally important. In this section, we'll explore how to test the accessibility of your Android app, identify common issues, and use tools to improve accessibility.

Why Test for Accessibility?

Testing for accessibility helps you identify and fix issues that might hinder users with disabilities from using your app effectively. Accessibility testing not only ensures compliance with accessibility standards but also enhances the user experience for a broader audience. By catching accessibility issues early in the development process, you can save time and effort in addressing them.

Manual Accessibility Testing

Manual testing involves evaluating your app's user interface and interactions to identify accessibility issues. Here are some key aspects to consider during manual accessibility testing:

1. **Navigation**: Verify that users can navigate through your app using screen readers and keyboard input. Check that all interactive elements, like buttons and links, can be accessed and activated without issues.

2. **Text Alternatives**: Ensure that all images, buttons, and other non-text elements have appropriate text alternatives. Screen readers rely on these descriptions to convey information to users.

3. **Color and Contrast**: Check the color contrast between text and background elements. Ensure that text is legible for users with low vision or color blindness.

4. **Focus Indicators**: Test the visibility of focus indicators when using keyboard navigation. Users should be able to clearly see which element has focus.

5. **Content Order**: Verify that the order in which content is presented is logical and follows a meaningful sequence. Screen readers read content in the order it appears in the accessibility tree.

6. **Form Fields**: Check that form fields are properly labeled, and input elements have clear and concise instructions.

7. **Testing with Assistive Technologies**: Use screen readers and other assistive technologies to interact with your app during testing. Familiarize yourself with how these tools work.

Automated Accessibility Testing

Automated accessibility testing tools can help identify common issues quickly. Android provides the Accessibility Scanner tool, which is a great resource for automated testing. Here's how to use it:

1. **Enable Accessibility Scanner**: Go to your device's Settings > Accessibility > Accessibility Scanner, and turn it on.

2. **Open Your App**: Launch your app and navigate through its various screens and interactions.

3. **Scan for Issues**: After using your app, open the Accessibility Scanner tool, and tap the "Accessibility Scanner" button to analyze the app's accessibility.

4. **Review and Fix Issues**: The tool will provide a list of issues and suggestions for improvement. Address these issues in your app's code and user interface.

Continuous Accessibility Testing

Integrate accessibility testing into your development workflow. Consider using continuous integration (CI) tools that run accessibility checks automatically whenever you make changes to your app's codebase. This ensures that accessibility is a consistent focus throughout the development process.

Conclusion

Testing for accessibility is a fundamental step in creating Android apps that are inclusive and user-friendly. By combining manual testing, automated tools like the Accessibility Scanner, and continuous testing practices, you can identify and address accessibility issues effectively. Making accessibility testing a routine part of your development process helps you reach a broader audience and provide a better user experience for everyone.

Section 18.4: Inclusive Design Principles

Inclusive design, also known as universal design, is an approach to creating products and environments that consider the needs of all people, regardless of their abilities, age, or other characteristics. In the context of Android app development, inclusive design principles are essential for creating applications that are accessible and usable by the widest possible audience. In this section, we'll explore key inclusive design principles and how to apply them to your Android app.

1. User-Centered Design

Start by understanding your users' needs and preferences. Conduct user research, gather feedback, and involve diverse user groups, including people with disabilities, in your design and testing processes. Prioritize user needs in your design decisions.

2. Clear and Consistent Navigation

Provide straightforward and consistent navigation paths within your app. Users, including those with disabilities, should easily understand how to move between different sections of your app. Use meaningful labels for buttons and navigation elements.

3. Readable and Understandable Content

Ensure that text content in your app is legible and comprehensible. Use readable fonts, appropriate font sizes, and sufficient contrast between text and background. Write clear and concise content, and avoid jargon or overly technical language.

4. Flexible Interaction

Design interactions that accommodate various input methods, such as touch, voice commands, and keyboard input. Avoid interactions that rely solely on gestures or precise touch targets, as these can be challenging for some users.

5. Accessible Images and Media

Provide alternative text descriptions for images and multimedia content. This is crucial for users who rely on screen readers to understand the visual elements of your app. Ensure that multimedia content includes captions and transcripts.

6. Keyboard and Voice Navigation

Support keyboard navigation for users who cannot use touch interfaces. Ensure that all interactive elements, including buttons and form fields, can be accessed and operated using a keyboard. Additionally, consider voice navigation and provide voice commands for essential app functions.

7. Testing with Assistive Technologies

Regularly test your app with assistive technologies such as screen readers, voice assistants, and switch devices. Familiarize yourself with how these tools work and how users with disabilities interact with your app. Address any issues that arise during testing promptly.

8. Progressive Disclosure

Present information and options progressively to prevent overwhelming users, especially those with cognitive disabilities. Use accordions, expandable sections, or step-by-step wizards to break down complex tasks into manageable steps.

9. Error Handling and Recovery

Design error messages that are clear and informative. Provide guidance on how users can correct errors, and avoid using technical language. Allow users to review and change their inputs before submitting forms or actions.

10. Flexibility in Display

Offer users options to customize the display settings, such as text size, color schemes, and contrast settings. This allows users to adapt the app to their specific needs and preferences.

11. Feedback and User Support

Include feedback mechanisms in your app to let users report issues or provide feedback. Ensure that customer support channels are accessible and responsive to user inquiries and concerns.

12. Continuous Improvement

Incorporate feedback and user testing results into your app's ongoing development. Regularly update your app to address accessibility issues and improve the user experience for all users.

By incorporating these inclusive design principles into your Android app development process, you can create applications that are not only accessible but also provide a better user experience for everyone. Inclusive design not only benefits users with disabilities but also enhances the overall usability and reach of your app.

Section 18.5: Promoting Inclusivity in Your Apps

Promoting inclusivity in your Android apps goes beyond adhering to accessibility guidelines; it's about creating a welcoming and supportive environment for all users. In this section, we'll explore strategies for promoting inclusivity in your apps, fostering a sense of belonging, and making users feel valued and respected.

1. Diverse Representation

Consider the diversity of your user base when selecting images, avatars, and other visual elements. Ensure that your app represents people from various backgrounds, ethnicities, genders, and abilities. This sends a message of inclusivity and makes all users feel recognized.

2. Inclusive Language

Use language that is neutral, respectful, and inclusive. Avoid gender-specific terms and pronouns unless necessary. Be mindful of cultural sensitivities and offensive language. Inclusive language fosters a sense of belonging and respect among users.

3. Community Building

Create opportunities for users to connect and build communities within your app. Features like discussion forums, user groups, or social networking can help users find like-minded individuals and support networks. Encourage positive interactions and discourage harassment or bullying.

4. Accessibility Feedback Loop

Establish a feedback loop for accessibility. Encourage users, especially those with disabilities, to provide feedback on accessibility issues or improvements they'd like to see. Act on this feedback promptly to demonstrate your commitment to inclusivity.

5. User Testing with Diverse Groups

Conduct user testing with a diverse group of participants. Include users with disabilities, users from different cultural backgrounds, and users of various ages and abilities. This can uncover usability issues and ensure your app meets the needs of a wide range of users.

6. Cultural Sensitivity

Respect cultural differences in your app's content and design. Avoid using symbols, images, or colors that may carry negative connotations in certain cultures. Consider internationalization and localization to make your app more accessible to global audiences.

7. Inclusive Marketing

Ensure that your marketing materials, including advertisements and promotional content, reflect the diversity and inclusivity of your user base. Use diverse imagery and messaging that speaks to a wide range of potential users.

8. Inclusive Design Workshops

Host inclusive design workshops within your development team. Encourage team members to think critically about inclusivity in the design and development process. Share resources and best practices to enhance everyone's understanding.

9. Inclusivity Statements

Consider including an inclusivity statement or commitment in your app's terms of service or about section. This statement can convey your dedication to inclusivity, privacy, and user rights.

10. Continuous Education

Stay informed about emerging best practices in inclusivity and accessibility. Attend workshops, conferences, and training sessions related to inclusive design. Share your knowledge with your team and peers.

11. Feedback Mechanisms

Implement accessible and straightforward feedback mechanisms within your app. Allow users to report issues related to inclusivity, harassment, or offensive content. Address these reports promptly and enforce community guidelines.

12. Regular Audits

Perform regular audits of your app's content and design to identify potential areas for improvement. Accessibility audits, content audits, and diversity audits can help you maintain a high standard of inclusivity.

13. Transparency and Accountability

Be transparent about your app's practices and data handling. Hold yourself accountable for any mistakes or lapses in inclusivity. Communicate openly with your user community.

Promoting inclusivity in your Android apps is an ongoing commitment. By fostering an inclusive environment, you can create apps that resonate with a wide audience, build a loyal user base, and contribute positively to a more inclusive digital ecosystem.

Chapter 19: Kotlin for Cross-Platform Development

Kotlin Multiplatform is a powerful tool for developers looking to write code that can run on multiple platforms, including Android and iOS. In this chapter, we'll delve into the world of cross-platform development with Kotlin, exploring how to share code, manage platform-specific implementations, and create truly cross-platform applications.

Section 19.1: Introduction to Kotlin Multiplatform

Kotlin Multiplatform, often abbreviated as KMP, is an exciting technology that allows you to write shared code that can be used across different platforms, such as Android, iOS, and even web applications. This approach not only reduces development time but also ensures consistency and minimizes the chances of bugs when implementing the same functionality on multiple platforms.

Key Concepts of Kotlin Multiplatform:

1. **Shared Code:** The core idea behind Kotlin Multiplatform is sharing code. You write common code in Kotlin, and this code can be reused across various platforms without modification.

2. **Platform-Specific Code:** While sharing code is a significant advantage, Kotlin Multiplatform allows you to write platform-specific code when necessary. This enables you to implement platform-specific features or utilize platform-specific APIs.

3. **Kotlin Everywhere:** With Kotlin Multiplatform, you can use Kotlin on all target platforms, whether it's Android, iOS (using Kotlin Native), or other environments where Kotlin is supported.

4. **Code Sharing Gradation:** Depending on your project's requirements, you can choose the level of code sharing that suits your needs. It can range from sharing only business logic to sharing UI components and more.

Kotlin Multiplatform Project Structure:

A typical Kotlin Multiplatform project has the following structure:

- **Shared Module:** Contains the shared Kotlin code that is intended to run on multiple platforms.
- **Platform-Specific Modules:** Separate modules for each platform (e.g., Android, iOS) where you write platform-specific code.
- **Build Configuration:** Gradle or other build configurations that define how shared and platform-specific code is compiled and linked.

Benefits of Kotlin Multiplatform:

1. **Code Reusability:** Share business logic, data models, and algorithms between platforms, reducing duplication.

2. **Consistency:** Ensure consistency in behavior and features across platforms.

3. **Time and Cost Savings:** Develop for multiple platforms simultaneously, saving time and development costs.

4. **Maintainability:** Changes made in shared code are reflected across all platforms, making maintenance more straightforward.

5. **Leverage Kotlin Features:** Benefit from Kotlin's concise syntax, type safety, and modern language features on all platforms.

In the following sections, we will explore the practical aspects of Kotlin Multiplatform, including setting up a project, sharing code, managing platform-specific implementations, and overcoming common challenges in cross-platform development.

Section 19.2: Sharing Code between Android and iOS

In Kotlin Multiplatform, one of the primary use cases is sharing code between Android and iOS platforms. This allows you to create cross-platform applications with shared business logic while still leveraging platform-specific features when needed. In this section, we'll dive into how you can effectively share code between these two major mobile platforms.

Kotlin Multiplatform Mobile (KMM)

To share code between Android and iOS, JetBrains has introduced Kotlin Multiplatform Mobile (KMM), a set of tools and libraries that facilitate cross-platform development. KMM streamlines the process of creating shared modules, handling dependencies, and integrating with platform-specific codebases.

To get started with KMM, you typically create a shared module within your project. This module contains the Kotlin code that you want to share across platforms. Here's an overview of the steps:

1. **Create a New KMM Module:** Use the appropriate KMM plugin or command-line tools to create a new shared module within your Android Studio or Xcode project.

2. **Define Shared Code:** Write your shared Kotlin code in this module. This can include data models, business logic, networking code, and more.

3. **Interoperability:** For platform-specific functionality or UI components, you can utilize Kotlin's interoperability features. For example, you can use Kotlin Native to interact with iOS-specific APIs.

4. **Dependency Management:** Dependencies specific to the shared module are managed within the module's Gradle (for Android) or Xcode project (for iOS).

Usage in Android and iOS Projects

Once you've defined your shared module, you can consume it in both your Android and iOS projects:

*   **Android:** In your Android project, you'll include the shared module as a dependency in your app's Gradle configuration. You can then access and use the shared Kotlin code as if it were part of your Android app.

*   **iOS:** In your iOS project, you'll link the shared module as a framework or library. This allows you to call shared Kotlin functions and use shared data structures from your Swift or Objective-C code.

Example Use Case

Imagine you're building a weather forecasting app for both Android and iOS. You can create a shared module that contains the weather data model, networking code for fetching weather information, and data parsing logic. Both Android and iOS can then use this shared code to display weather forecasts in their respective user interfaces.

Here's a simplified example of shared code for fetching weather data:

```kotlin
// SharedModule.kt (Kotlin Multiplatform Shared Module)

data class WeatherForecast(val temperature: Double, val condition: String)

expect class WeatherApi() {
    suspend fun getWeather(location: String): WeatherForecast
}
```

In this example, the WeatherApi class declares an expected function getWeather() that should be implemented differently on Android and iOS. On Android, you'd use Android-specific networking libraries like Retrofit, while on iOS, you'd use native networking APIs. The shared data class WeatherForecast represents the weather data structure that is used on both platforms.

This is just a glimpse of how Kotlin Multiplatform allows you to share code while still accommodating platform-specific differences. In practice, you can share a wide range of code, from UI components to complex business logic, making cross-platform development more efficient and consistent.

Section 19.3: Building Desktop Applications with Kotlin

While Kotlin is well-known for its application in Android and mobile development, it is also a versatile language for building desktop applications. In this section, we'll explore how you can leverage Kotlin to create cross-platform desktop applications with user interfaces (UIs).

Kotlin Desktop Applications

Kotlin allows you to build desktop applications for various platforms, including Windows, macOS, and Linux, using different libraries and frameworks. Some popular choices for Kotlin desktop development include:

- **JavaFX:** Kotlin can be seamlessly used with JavaFX to create rich desktop applications with graphical user interfaces. JavaFX provides a comprehensive set of UI controls and layout options.

- **TornadoFX:** TornadoFX is a Kotlin-centric library built on top of JavaFX. It simplifies UI development by providing a more Kotlin-esque API for creating JavaFX-based applications.

- **Swing:** Kotlin can also be used with Swing, a long-standing Java library for building desktop GUIs. While Swing may not have the modern look and feel of JavaFX, it is still a viable option for cross-platform desktop applications.

Cross-Platform Desktop Development

One of the strengths of Kotlin for desktop development is its cross-platform compatibility. You can write your Kotlin desktop application code once and run it on multiple platforms without major modifications.

To achieve cross-platform compatibility, follow these steps:

1. **Use a Cross-Platform UI Library:** Choose a UI library or framework that supports multiple platforms. JavaFX, TornadoFX, and Swing are good options for this purpose.

2. **Write Platform-Independent Code:** When writing the core logic of your application, focus on platform-independent Kotlin code. Avoid platform-specific dependencies as much as possible.

3. **Handle Platform-Specific Differences:** In some cases, you may need to address platform-specific differences. Use conditional compilation and platform-specific modules to isolate platform-specific code.

Example Code

Let's consider a simple example of a cross-platform desktop application that displays "Hello, Kotlin Desktop!" in a window. We'll use JavaFX for this illustration:

```kotlin
import javafx.application.Application
import javafx.scene.Scene
import javafx.scene.control.Label
import javafx.scene.layout.StackPane
import javafx.stage.Stage

class HelloWorldApp : Application() {
    override fun start(primaryStage: Stage) {
        val root = StackPane()
        val label = Label("Hello, Kotlin Desktop!")
        root.children.add(label)

        val scene = Scene(root, 300.0, 200.0)
        primaryStage.title = "Kotlin Desktop App"
        primaryStage.scene = scene

        primaryStage.show()
    }
}

fun main() {
    Application.launch(HelloWorldApp::class.java)
}
```

In this code, we create a basic JavaFX application using Kotlin. It's important to note that this code can be easily adapted to work on multiple desktop platforms with minimal changes.

Distribution and Deployment

When it comes to distributing and deploying your Kotlin desktop application, you can package it as a JAR file, an EXE file (Windows), a DMG file (macOS), or a DEB/RPM package (Linux). Each platform has its own packaging and deployment tools.

Kotlin's flexibility, combined with cross-platform UI libraries, makes it a compelling choice for desktop application development, enabling you to target a wide range of users across different operating systems with a single codebase.

Section 19.4: Web Development with Kotlin/JS

Kotlin's versatility extends beyond Android, desktop, and server-side development; it can also be used for web development. Kotlin/JS is a subset of Kotlin that transpiles into JavaScript, making it suitable for building web applications. In this section, we'll delve into Kotlin/JS and explore how you can leverage it to create interactive web applications.

Kotlin/JS Basics

Kotlin/JS enables you to write Kotlin code that runs in web browsers alongside JavaScript. Here's a brief overview of Kotlin/JS:

- **Transpilation:** Kotlin/JS code is transpiled into JavaScript, which can be executed in web browsers. This transpilation process ensures cross-browser compatibility.

- **Interop:** Kotlin/JS allows seamless interoperation with existing JavaScript libraries and code. You can use JavaScript libraries like React, Vue.js, or any other web framework within your Kotlin/JS project.

- **Strong Typing:** Kotlin brings its strong typing system to the web. This helps catch type-related errors during development, reducing runtime issues.

Setting Up a Kotlin/JS Project

To get started with Kotlin/JS, you need to set up a project. Here are the basic steps:

1. **Install Kotlin:** Ensure you have Kotlin installed on your system. You can download it from the official website or use a build tool like Gradle or Maven to manage Kotlin dependencies.

2. **Create a Kotlin/JS Project:** Use the Kotlin command-line tools or your preferred build tool to create a new Kotlin/JS project.

3. **Write Kotlin/JS Code:** Start writing Kotlin code for your web application. You can create web components, handle user interactions, and define the application's logic.

4. **Transpile to JavaScript:** Use the Kotlin compiler or build tool to transpile your Kotlin code into JavaScript.

5. **HTML and CSS:** Create HTML and CSS files to structure and style your web application's user interface. You can also use templating engines like Kotlinx.html.

6. **Run in a Browser:** Open your HTML file in a web browser to test your Kotlin/JS web application.

Example Code

Here's a simple Kotlin/JS example that creates an interactive button on a web page:

```kotlin
import kotlinx.browser.document
import org.w3c.dom.HTMLButtonElement

fun main() {
    val button = document.createElement("button") as HTMLButtonElement
    button.textContent = "Click Me"
    button.addEventListener("click", {
        button.textContent = "Hello, Kotlin/JS!"
    })

    document.body?.appendChild(button)
}
```

In this code, we import the document object from kotlinx.browser, which represents the web page's DOM. We create an HTML button element, add a click event listener to it, and change its text content when clicked.

Libraries and Frameworks

Kotlin/JS can be used with various libraries and frameworks to build web applications. Some popular choices include:

- **Kotlin React:** A Kotlin wrapper for the React JavaScript library, which is widely used for building user interfaces.

- **Ktor:** A Kotlin-native asynchronous web framework that can be used for both server-side and client-side web development.

- **Kotlin/JS Wrappers:** Many JavaScript libraries and frameworks have Kotlin/JS wrappers, making it easy to use them in your Kotlin/JS projects.

Packaging and Deployment

Once your Kotlin/JS web application is ready, you can package and deploy it just like any other web application. This may involve bundling your JavaScript code, optimizing assets, and hosting the application on a web server or a cloud platform.

Kotlin/JS opens up exciting possibilities for web development, allowing you to leverage Kotlin's language features and interoperate with existing JavaScript libraries while building modern and robust web applications.

Section 19.5: Case Studies in Cross-Platform Development

In this section, we will explore real-world case studies of cross-platform development using Kotlin Multiplatform. Kotlin Multiplatform is a powerful technology that enables code sharing between different platforms, such as Android and iOS, while maintaining native performance and user experience. These case studies will highlight the versatility and advantages of Kotlin Multiplatform for various types of applications.

Case Study 1: Mobile Banking App

Problem: A financial institution wants to create a mobile banking app that is available on both Android and iOS platforms. They need a cost-effective solution that allows them to maintain a single codebase for core functionality while ensuring a native look and feel on each platform.

Solution: Kotlin Multiplatform is used to write the core business logic of the banking app, including user authentication, transaction processing, and account management. Platform-specific UI components and navigation are implemented using native Android and iOS development tools. This approach reduces development time and ensures consistency across platforms.

```kotlin
// Shared Kotlin Multiplatform code for transaction processing
expect class TransactionProcessor() {
    fun processTransaction(amount: Double)
}

// Android-specific implementation
actual class AndroidTransactionProcessor : TransactionProcessor() {
    override fun processTransaction(amount: Double) {
        // Implement Android-specific transaction processing
    }
}

// iOS-specific implementation
actual class iOSTransactionProcessor : TransactionProcessor() {
    override fun processTransaction(amount: Double) {
        // Implement iOS-specific transaction processing
    }
}
```

Case Study 2: e-Commerce App

Problem: An e-commerce company wants to expand its reach by offering its shopping app on both Android and iOS platforms. They need a solution that allows them to share the product catalog, shopping cart, and payment processing logic between the two platforms.

Solution: Kotlin Multiplatform is used to create shared modules for product catalog management, shopping cart functionality, and payment processing. These modules are included in both the Android and iOS versions of the app. Platform-specific code handles UI, navigation, and integration with payment gateways.

```kotlin
// Shared Kotlin Multiplatform code for product catalog
class Product(val id: String, val name: String, val price: Double)

// Shared shopping cart logic
class ShoppingCart {
    private val items: MutableList<Product> = mutableListOf()
```

```
    fun addItem(product: Product) {
        items.add(product)
    }

    // Other shopping cart methods...
}
```

Case Study 3: Social Media Integration

Problem: A social media startup wants to build a cross-platform app that integrates with various social media platforms, such as Facebook, Twitter, and Instagram. They aim to minimize duplicate code and maintenance effort.

Solution: Kotlin Multiplatform is used to create shared modules for social media authentication and interaction. These modules provide a unified API for logging in, posting content, and accessing user profiles across different platforms. Platform-specific implementations handle the nuances of each social media API.

```
// Shared Kotlin Multiplatform code for social media integration
expect class SocialMediaClient() {
    suspend fun login()
    suspend fun postToFeed(content: String)
    suspend fun getUserProfile(): UserProfile
}

// Android-specific implementation
actual class AndroidSocialMediaClient : SocialMediaClient() {
    // Implement Android-specific social media integration
}

// iOS-specific implementation
actual class iOSSocialMediaClient : SocialMediaClient() {
    // Implement iOS-specific social media integration
}
```

These case studies illustrate the flexibility and advantages of Kotlin Multiplatform for cross-platform development. Whether you're building a mobile banking app, an e-commerce platform, or integrating with social media, Kotlin Multiplatform allows you to share code efficiently while delivering a native experience on each platform. It streamlines development, reduces duplication, and accelerates time-to-market for your cross-platform applications.

Chapter 20: Future Trends and Emerging Technologies

Section 20.1: Exploring Emerging Android Technologies

In this section, we'll delve into the exciting world of emerging Android technologies that are shaping the future of mobile development. As the Android ecosystem evolves, developers need to stay informed about the latest trends and innovations to build cutting-edge apps that leverage new capabilities and provide enhanced user experiences.

1. 5G Connectivity

One of the most significant advancements in mobile technology is the rollout of 5G networks. 5G offers faster download and upload speeds, lower latency, and increased network capacity compared to 4G. As a developer, understanding the potential of 5G is crucial. It enables real-time communication, high-quality video streaming, and immersive AR/VR experiences. Optimizing your apps for 5G can give you a competitive edge.

2. Augmented Reality (AR) and Virtual Reality (VR)

AR and VR technologies continue to gain traction in the Android ecosystem. ARCore and ARKit have made it easier to develop augmented reality apps that overlay digital content onto the real world. VR headsets like Oculus Quest provide immersive experiences. Consider how AR and VR can enhance your apps, from gaming and education to interior design and remote collaboration.

3. Foldable and Dual-Screen Devices

Foldable and dual-screen devices offer new form factors for Android apps. Devices like the Samsung Galaxy Z Fold and Microsoft Surface Duo challenge developers to create responsive layouts and utilize multiple screens effectively. Explore how your apps can take advantage of these innovative devices for improved multitasking and user experiences.

4. Machine Learning and AI

Machine learning and AI are becoming increasingly accessible to Android developers. ML Kit, TensorFlow Lite, and other frameworks empower you to integrate machine learning models into your apps for tasks like image recognition, natural language processing, and predictive analytics. AI-driven personalization and recommendations can boost user engagement.

5. Internet of Things (IoT) Integration

IoT is extending its reach into the Android ecosystem. Android Things and other platforms enable developers to build apps that control smart home devices, industrial sensors, and wearable gadgets. Consider how your apps can leverage IoT data and interactions to provide valuable services and automation.

6. Privacy and Security

As data privacy concerns grow, Android continues to enhance user privacy and security. Stay updated on changes to permissions, data collection policies, and security best practices. Protecting user data and earning their trust is essential for the long-term success of your apps.

7. App Architecture and Performance Optimization

Efficient app architecture and performance optimization are timeless trends. Jetpack Compose, Kotlin Coroutines, and other tools are evolving to simplify app development while maintaining high performance. Stay informed about best practices for building responsive, smooth, and efficient apps.

In this rapidly evolving landscape, keeping up with emerging technologies is essential for Android developers. Whether you're building consumer apps, enterprise solutions, or games, embracing these trends can open up new possibilities and ensure your apps remain relevant and competitive. In the subsequent sections of this chapter, we'll dive deeper into specific emerging technologies like AR/VR integration, 5G, quantum computing, and more.

Section 20.2: AR/VR Integration in Android

In this section, we'll explore the integration of Augmented Reality (AR) and Virtual Reality (VR) technologies into Android applications. AR and VR have gained significant traction in recent years, offering immersive experiences that go beyond traditional mobile app interactions. These technologies have the potential to revolutionize various industries, from gaming and education to healthcare and architecture.

ARCore and ARKit

ARCore for Android and ARKit for iOS are development platforms that enable the creation of augmented reality experiences. They provide APIs for detecting and tracking real-world objects and surfaces, as well as rendering virtual objects within the user's environment. ARCore and ARKit have made it easier for developers to build AR apps without extensive knowledge of computer vision.

To get started with AR integration, you'll need to:

1. **Install AR SDKs**: Add ARCore or ARKit SDK to your project, depending on the platform you're targeting. These SDKs provide the necessary tools and libraries for AR development.

2. **Understand Tracking**: Learn how to use AR tracking to detect surfaces and objects. This is essential for placing virtual content accurately in the real world.

3. **3D Modeling**: Create or import 3D models of virtual objects that you want to place in the AR environment.

4. **User Interaction**: Implement interactions that allow users to interact with AR objects, such as tapping, dragging, or scaling.

5. **Optimization**: Ensure your AR app runs smoothly by optimizing performance. AR experiences can be resource-intensive, so efficient rendering is crucial.

Use Cases for AR Integration

AR integration opens up a wide range of use cases, including:

1. Gaming: Create games where virtual characters or objects interact with the player's surroundings. Pokémon GO is a classic example of AR gaming.

2. Education: Develop educational apps that provide interactive lessons using AR. For instance, students can explore historical events by viewing 3D recreations.

3. Navigation: Implement AR navigation apps that overlay directions and points of interest onto the real world, simplifying navigation.

4. Retail: Enhance the online shopping experience by allowing users to visualize products in their real environment before making a purchase.

5. Interior Design: Help users visualize how furniture or decor items would look in their home through AR interior design apps.

Virtual Reality (VR)

While AR augments the real world, VR immerses users in entirely virtual environments. To integrate VR into Android apps, you can use platforms like Google VR or Oculus for more specialized experiences.

VR development involves:

1. **Choosing a VR Platform**: Select a VR platform that suits your app's requirements, such as Google Cardboard, Oculus Quest, or Daydream.

2. **Creating VR Content**: Design virtual environments, 3D models, and interactive elements for your VR app.

3. **User Input**: Implement VR interactions using gaze-based input, controllers, or hand tracking, depending on the VR hardware.

4. **Performance Optimization**: VR applications demand high performance to maintain a smooth and comfortable experience. Optimize rendering and reduce latency.

Use Cases for VR Integration

VR integration can be beneficial in various domains, including:

1. Gaming: *Develop immersive games where users can explore virtual worlds and interact with objects.*

2. Training and Simulations: *Use VR for training simulations, such as flight training or medical simulations.*

3. Virtual Tours: *Create virtual tours for real estate, travel, or museums, allowing users to explore places and artifacts from the comfort of their homes.*

4. Healthcare: *Implement VR therapies and pain management techniques, offering an alternative to traditional treatments.*

5. Design and Architecture: *Architects and designers can use VR to walk clients through virtual building designs, providing a realistic preview.*

The integration of AR and VR technologies offers exciting opportunities for Android developers. Whether you're looking to create captivating games, educational experiences, or innovative solutions for industries, mastering AR/VR development can be a valuable skill in the future of Android app development.

Section 20.3: 5G and IoT Revolution

In this section, we'll delve into the impact of 5G (fifth-generation) wireless technology and the Internet of Things (IoT) on the future of Android development. These two technologies are poised to transform how Android apps are built, used, and experienced.

5G: The Next Generation of Connectivity

5G is not just an incremental upgrade from 4G; it represents a significant leap in wireless technology. With 5G, we can expect:

1. Blazing Fast Speeds: 5G promises ultra-fast download and upload speeds, reducing latency significantly. This will enable applications that rely on real-time data, such as augmented reality, virtual reality, and cloud gaming.

2. Enhanced Connectivity: The vast number of devices that can be connected per square kilometer will increase. This opens up opportunities for large-scale IoT deployments and more seamless connectivity in crowded areas.

3. Edge Computing: 5G's low latency makes edge computing more feasible. This means processing data closer to the source, reducing the need for data to travel to distant data centers. Android apps can benefit from faster, localized processing.

4. IoT Acceleration: The speed and low latency of 5G are pivotal for IoT applications. Smart homes, industrial automation, autonomous vehicles, and healthcare systems will all benefit from reliable, high-speed connectivity.

To leverage 5G in your Android apps, consider the following:

- **Network Awareness**: Design apps that can adapt to changing network conditions. For example, you might prioritize data synchronization or content delivery differently based on whether the device is on 5G, 4G, or Wi-Fi.

- **Low-Latency Features**: Explore real-time communication, gaming, and interactive applications that harness 5G's low-latency capabilities.

- **Edge Computing**: Investigate the integration of edge computing for your apps to offload processing to nearby servers, improving response times.

The Internet of Things (IoT)

The IoT involves connecting everyday objects and devices to the internet, enabling them to collect and exchange data. This interconnected ecosystem holds immense potential for Android developers:

1. IoT Devices: Android apps can interact with a wide array of IoT devices, including smart appliances, wearables, sensors, and more. These devices provide opportunities for data collection, remote control, and automation.

2. Data Analytics: IoT generates vast amounts of data. Android apps can play a crucial role in processing and visualizing this data, providing actionable insights to users.

3. Home Automation: Develop apps that allow users to control and monitor their smart homes. This can include lighting, climate control, security systems, and more.

4. Industrial IoT: Android apps can be used in industrial settings to monitor machinery, track inventory, and optimize processes through IoT sensors and devices.

To work with IoT in Android development:

- **IoT Protocols**: Familiarize yourself with IoT communication protocols such as MQTT, CoAP, or HTTP, depending on the devices you're connecting to.

- **Security**: IoT security is paramount. Ensure your Android apps have robust security measures in place, especially when handling sensitive data from IoT devices.

- **Compatibility**: Consider the diversity of IoT devices and ensure your apps are compatible with various brands and models.

The combination of 5G and IoT opens up a new world of possibilities for Android developers. As these technologies continue to evolve, staying updated and exploring innovative use cases will be key to creating cutting-edge Android applications. Whether you're developing consumer-facing apps or solutions for industries, the 5G and IoT revolution will play a pivotal role in shaping the future of Android development.

Section 20.4: Quantum Computing and Android

In this section, we'll explore the intriguing intersection of quantum computing and Android development. Quantum computing represents a paradigm shift in computation that has the potential to transform various industries, including mobile app development.

Understanding Quantum Computing

Before delving into its implications for Android, let's briefly understand what quantum computing is:

- **Quantum Bits (Qubits)**: Unlike classical bits, which can be either 0 or 1, qubits can exist in multiple states simultaneously due to a phenomenon called superposition. This property allows quantum computers to perform certain calculations exponentially faster than classical computers.

- **Quantum Entanglement**: Qubits can become entangled, meaning the state of one qubit is linked to the state of another, even when they are physically separated. This property enables quantum computers to solve complex problems that were previously impractical.

- **Quantum Supremacy**: Quantum computers have achieved "quantum supremacy" by performing calculations that are practically impossible for classical computers to replicate within a reasonable time frame.

Quantum Computing and Android

So, how does quantum computing intersect with Android development? Here are some key points to consider:

1. Quantum Algorithms: *Quantum computing can potentially lead to the development of new algorithms that dramatically enhance the performance of Android apps. For instance, quantum algorithms may optimize data processing, encryption, and artificial intelligence tasks.*

2. Security: *Quantum computing poses both opportunities and challenges in terms of security. While quantum-resistant encryption algorithms will be necessary to protect Android apps and user data, quantum cryptography could provide ultra-secure communication channels.*

3. Simulation: *Quantum computers excel at simulating quantum systems, which is crucial in fields like chemistry, materials science, and drug discovery. Android apps may leverage quantum simulation to provide real-time insights in these domains.*

4. Optimization: *Quantum computers can tackle optimization problems efficiently. Android apps dealing with logistics, scheduling, and resource allocation could benefit from quantum-powered optimization.*

5. Quantum Cloud Services: *Quantum computing is likely to become available through cloud services. Android developers may access quantum computing resources to execute tasks that require quantum capabilities.*

Preparing for Quantum Integration

While quantum computing is still in its infancy, Android developers can take some steps to prepare for its integration:

- **Stay Informed**: Keep abreast of developments in quantum computing and how they apply to your app domain.

- **Quantum Libraries**: Familiarize yourself with quantum programming languages and libraries that may become relevant in the future.

- **Security Measures**: Plan for quantum-resistant cryptography to ensure data security in a post-quantum world.

- **Partnerships**: Consider collaborations with organizations at the forefront of quantum computing to explore potential synergies.

Quantum computing holds the promise of revolutionizing computation, and as Android developers, being adaptable and forward-thinking will be essential in harnessing its potential. While quantum integration in Android apps may be on the horizon, it's an exciting and evolving field that is worth monitoring.

Section 20.5: The Next Decade of Android Development

As we look forward to the future of Android development, several exciting trends and advancements are likely to shape the next decade of this dynamic field. In this section, we'll explore some key areas that developers should keep an eye on.

1. AI and Machine Learning Integration**

Artificial Intelligence (AI) and Machine Learning (ML) are expected to play an even more prominent role in Android development. With tools like TensorFlow and ML Kit, developers can easily integrate AI capabilities into their apps for tasks such as image recognition, natural language processing, and predictive analytics. As AI hardware and algorithms advance, expect more AI-driven features in Android apps.

2. Foldable and Dual-Screen Devices**

The era of foldable and dual-screen Android devices is here to stay. Developers will need to adapt their apps to provide seamless user experiences across different screen configurations. These innovative devices offer new possibilities for multitasking and creative app design.

3. 5G Connectivity**

The rollout of 5G networks will revolutionize mobile app experiences. Android apps can harness the higher bandwidth and lower latency of 5G for real-time streaming, augmented reality (AR), and virtual reality (VR) applications. Developers should explore how their apps can take advantage of this transformative technology.

4. Privacy and Security**

Privacy and data security will remain paramount. Android developers will need to stay up-to-date with evolving privacy regulations and implement robust security measures to protect user data. The Android ecosystem is continually enhancing its security features, and developers should leverage these tools to build trust with users.

5. Cross-Platform Development**

Cross-platform development frameworks like Kotlin Multiplatform and Flutter will continue to gain popularity. These frameworks enable developers to write code once and deploy it on both Android and iOS platforms, saving time and resources. Expect increased adoption of cross-platform approaches.

6. Progressive Web Apps (PWAs)**

Progressive Web Apps, which combine the best of web and native apps, will become more prevalent. PWAs offer offline functionality, fast loading times, and a seamless user experience. Android developers should explore how to create PWAs and reach users across various platforms.

7. Augmented Reality (AR) and Virtual Reality (VR)**

AR and VR applications are becoming increasingly accessible on Android devices. Developers can create immersive experiences, from AR games to VR simulations. As AR and VR hardware evolves, these technologies will play a more significant role in the Android ecosystem.

8. Accessibility and Inclusivity**

Building apps that are accessible to all users, including those with disabilities, will be a fundamental requirement. Developers should follow accessibility best practices and ensure their apps are usable by everyone.

9. Sustainable Development**

Sustainability and eco-friendliness will gain importance. Android developers can contribute by optimizing their apps for energy efficiency and reducing environmental impact.

10. Community and Collaboration**

The Android development community will continue to grow, fostering collaboration and knowledge sharing. Developers should actively participate in communities, attend conferences, and contribute to open-source projects to stay connected and updated.

As we embark on the next decade of Android development, it's essential to remain adaptable, curious, and eager to embrace new technologies and trends. The Android platform is continually evolving, offering endless opportunities for innovation and creativity. Developers who stay informed and actively engage with the Android ecosystem will thrive in this exciting journey.

www.ingramcontent.com/pod-product-compliance
Lightning Source LLC
LaVergne TN
LVHW051325050326
832903LV00031B/3362